Sam Gardener

PORTRAIT OF ASHDOWN FOREST

By the same author

Portrait of the River Medway

Portrait of ASHDOWN FOREST

ROGER PENN

ROBERT HALE · LONDON

To my black cat, Charlie, who also loves forests

© *Roger Penn 1984*
First published in Great Britain 1984

ISBN 0 7090 1219 5

Robert Hale Limited
Clerkenwell House
Clerkenwell Green
London EC1R 0HT

Photoset in Century Schoolbook by
Kelly Typesetting Limited
Bradford-on-Avon, Wiltshire
Printed in Great Britain by
St Edmundsbury Press
Bury St Edmunds, Suffolk
Bound by Woolnough Bookbinding Limited

Contents

List of Illustrations

MAPS

PICTURE CREDITS

The author and publishers thank the following for permission to reproduce illustrations: Mr R. Montague, Forest Ranger and Mrs Montague (nos. 13, 14, 16, 18, 19, 27, 28, 29, 31, 36); Mr Alan Morriss, Pippingford Park (no. 22). All other photographs were taken by the author.

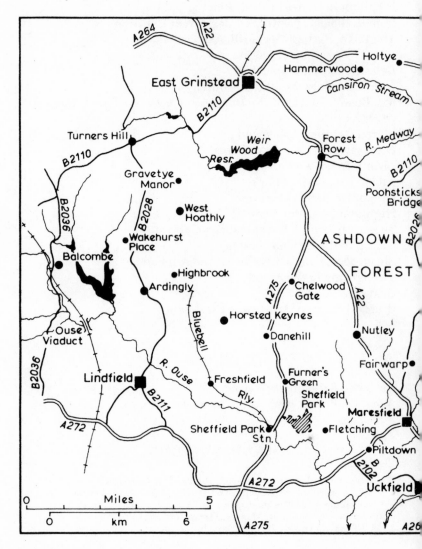

Ashdown Forest in its setting

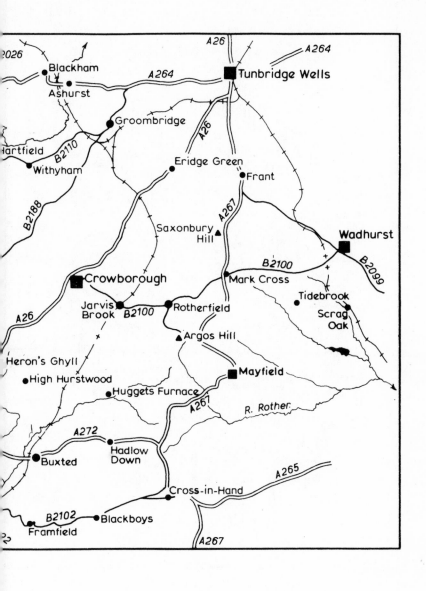

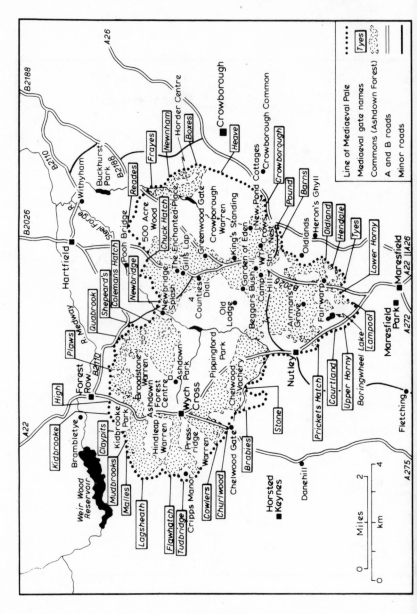

Ashdown Forest, with its medieval gate names

1

The Wealden Forest

Ashdown Forest in Sussex is the highest part of the Forest Ridges—those still well-wooded sandstone hills of the High Weald, which seen from afar can sometimes evoke an image of the great Wealden Forest.

This was a huge greenwood, dominated by oak and beech, which flourished for thousands of years in an almost unbroken sweep across Southern England, and in past millennia spread even over the dry land of what is now the North Sea and across the Channel bed into Northern France. Today its vast natural canopy of trees has shrunk to the open expanse of Ashdown and the smaller forests of Worth, St Leonard's, and the tiny relic of Waterdowne or Broadwater near Tunbridge Wells. Surviving remnants may exist at Gravetye, near West Hoathly; in Kent at Mereworth and at Wanden, near Pluckley. But a thousand years of gradual though determined clearance by man, fire and grazing animals have reduced and changed this once massive wildwood to mere patches.

Ashdown Forest itself is now a mosaic of high open heathland: dry, damp and wet, dotted with oak-birch woodland and attractive odd clumps of pine. Its landscape is deeply carved into wooded ravines, or ghylls, from which flow the many head-streams of the Medway and the Ouse. Among these features are larger tracts of woodland wherein lie several secluded private lakes, and the whole region gradually passes into the forested ridges and slopes of the High Weald. However, for most of the Wealden Forest's long history Ashdown Forest was simply part of the larger whole, distinguishable only by its height and its lightly wooded crests, and until the thirteenth century it was not even called Ashdown.

This history of this great forest cover of the Weald is really a series of episodes beginning after the retreat of the glaciers, until the forest gradually grew undisturbed to a natural climax. With the coming of Neolithic Man the forest began to be destroyed and its character changed; much later the Saxon and Jutish clearances started in earnest. Then came the Norman deer parks, medieval settlements and Tudor industry, followed by a Renaissance in the form of parkland and wooded estates which in turn led into Victorian arable farming. Finally today one finds modern conifer plantations and conservation of the remaining hardwoods.

Of course we could go back much further into geological time—in fact some two million years to the Late Pliocene—and glimpse Southern England before the onset of the Ice Ages. What we would see would in fact be not greatly different from now, either climatically or in the plant life, except for a few conifers which are not now native to Britain.

However, the Ice Ages destroyed all these primeval trees as the glaciers crept slowly southwards, and although there were long warm intervals between the six (or more) icy periods in which plants flourished again, they died each time the ice advanced again once more.

So, effectively, the Wealden Forest began its slow growth about 12,000 years ago in the closing stages of the glacial period we now call the Devensian. The Weald itself, lying south of the ice front, escaped actual glaciation, but it could not escape the cold and its climate was arctic-like and very dry. This Wealden land that was later to be covered in luxuriant forest was now a great open space of tufts of short grass and scrubby heath plants, relieved only by its bright flowering herbs during the short summer. The whole landscape was a type of bleak, park-like Tundra with dwarf willows, hardy birches and occasional clumps of juniper—not such an attractive landscape for the Late Old Stone Age hunters who had wandered in search of game far northwards from their warmer southern European caves across the wide isthmus to a bleak Britain.

Then for a few hundred years things got better and warmer, and the Weald saw its first real woodland with pine and birches; but the warmth did not last long enough to produce deciduous trees, for once more the cold returned with ice in the Scottish Highlands and Tundra in the south.

About 10,000 years ago the real warming-up began and into the south came birch and pine once more bringing open woodland, but it was a slow and gradual process. However, another long millennium brought a rather sudden change to warmth and dryness, the hazel replaced the birch and over from France came the oak and elm; later it became warm enough for the lime, even now the tallest broad-leaved tree in Britain—when we do not mutilate it by lopping.

Time passed and 7,500 years ago the climate changed again— still warm, but now much damper with the sea winds bringing rain. The sea level had slowly risen and it was about this time that Britain became an island. Almost the whole country was now densely forested. The climate, at least in the south, was at its peak, known as the Atlantic Phase or Climatic Optimum, and throughout the Weald and on the Downs there was a rich natural forest of mixed oak, alder and lime.

Then 5,000 years ago came a decline as the climate swung back to being drier and colder and with it came the Neolithic Revolution, or New Stone Age, when Man began to alter and thin the forests. Trees began to disappear from the South Downs when the first crops were sown on the chalklands. With them came the first weeds spreading along the edges of the early forest clearances, and the lime faded from the Wealden scene which changed to oak, alder and birch forest.

This period passed into the Bronze Age, and at its close came our present climate, sometimes called sub-Atlantic: basically cool and damp. This has persisted along with its ups and downs to the present day. Beech and hornbeam spread into the Weald, although not far beyond its borders, and with the chalklands now being abandoned the beech soon colonized them, while Man's metal tools and ploughs began to clear other wooded areas.

In 600 BC the Iron Age Celts arrived and remained undisturbed until AD 43. Their arrival coincided with another climatic downturn making the hazel tree important for scarce food. It was Celts who gave the Wealden Forest its first name— Coit Andred.

Then came the Romans, followed by a sunnier climate, so that the bright green of their vines adorned many a Wealden valley. They advanced into the surviving forest, which they called Silva Anderida, especially around Ashdown and the High Weald; they made roads for transporting the iron that was being mined there and the corn that was being grown on the South Downs and in North Kent (along with the weeds the corn brought like the scarlet pimpernel and the corn marigold).

With the departure of the Romans that confused period of history known as the Dark Ages was ushered in and much abandoned farmland reverted to secondary forest. The Teutonic invaders that took the Romans' place had at first been contracted mercenaries and licensed immigrants, but they now moved inland to the fringes of the Forest, and the real task of clearance began with the Saxons and Jutes on either side of the wooded barrier—their Andredsweald.

This led to rather different attitudes between the South Saxons of Sussex, and the Jutes or Frankish people of Kent. In Jutish Kent for the next three centuries the pattern was to leave the Forest in its original state and use it as vast commons, known as dens, where great herds of pigs got fat on acorns and beechmast. These commons were part of larger units called lathes, each with its Royal vill or township. So we can picture the Jutish Weald as a forest empty except in late spring and summer when cattle, came to graze, and then in the autumn when it became crowded with vast numbers of herded swine driven in from the outlying freeholdings. The Jutes were no miners and ignored the Wealden iron deposits, but they used the Roman roads, tracks and clearings. They could not cultivate the Clay Vale of Kent for it was waterlogged and barren, especially in its middle where the rivers of the Medway, Teise and Beult all joined to make a marshy delta dotted with trees. So their settlement of the Forest was quite a scattered one at river gaps and along the Greensand Ridge, and down their enormously broad droving routes; but there were few bridges, only fords. However, by the middle of the medieval period these vast herds of pigs and their pannage had faded away, and the Forest came to be used for its valuable timber.

In Sussex the landscape seemed at first to the South Saxons to be like their native Friesland or Saxony, and from their early settlements on the coast they pushed into the Low Weald. The new settlements became large villages, or manors, and their summer grazing clearings later changed to isolated farms. We have a good record of this early advance into the Forest because in 675 the Manor of Stanmer, south of Lewes, had swine pastures at Ardingly, Lindfield and West Hoathly.

However, it must have been hard and heavy going because these sodden, leaden Weald clays took hundreds of years to become fertile, and a vision of this has come down to us through an early Saxon poet, who wrote of "Har holtes feond" referring to the Saxon ploughman cultivating the edge of the forest and penetrating into it: "the old enemy of the wood—the ploughman".

What is interesting is that much of this woodland clearance of the later eighth and ninth centuries was not on virgin land at all, but recovered the "lost" farmland abandoned earlier during the Dark Ages which had probably reverted to a more tangled growth of secondary forest. Clearing was not only by fire and axe, but also by that universal eater of anything and everything—the goat. Goats needed little looking after, and were tough, hardy and easily domesticated, not bothered by enemies and rewarded their master by giving milk over a long period.

The Norman Conquest naturally brought change to the Weald, although the clearing of the forest continued, because the Normans' main effort was to organize the clearances for arable farming and to preserve as much as possible of the forest for multiple use like game, deer, cattle on the lines of a stratified society, thoroughly ordered and controlled. It is said that the Royal Forests came about through William I being so appalled at the lack of trees in England!

By the early Middle Ages this pioneering was almost over, and the forest timber was being used as a crop by the establishment of the ancient woodland arts of coppicing and pollarding, the first to get straight wood and the second to protect and lengthen a tree's life.

And so in the thirteenth century those who lived on the fringe of the Wealden Forest worked at all manner of woodland trades, from carpentry to basketmaking. One very important trade was centred around the yew tree. These were the bowyers and fletchers, bow and arrow makers, whose raw material was the basis of the medieval armaments industry.

One hundred years on and the Weald was in great contrast to the rest of the country, for less than a fifth of Britain's original tree cover was left. In the middle of the fourteenth century the Black Death swept over the land wiping out many from an under-nourished population still suffering from an earlier famine and crop failure caused by a sudden downturn in the climate. Ironically this setback probably saved a great deal of Wealden timber for by the fifteenth century there was a surplus. Much of this went from the old port of Winchelsea to London and Flanders, and there was a flourishing trade with the Nether-lands in oak bark for tanning.

Then in Tudor times occurred one of those great contrasts in English history, for although England was still an empty land, with much fen and heath and great flocks of now vanished birds on the open Downland, inside the Weald there was a growing iron industry. Dozens of books have often, and quite wrongly, singled it out as the prodigal son of the Weald in its use of timber for charcoal, which of course was in heavy demand for many other trades like clothing and shipbuilding. But in truth the wood was coppiced from many different trees, not just oaks; in any case, oaks were by law coppiced with standards giving a great growth of underwood, and which after ten, or twelve, years could be used for fuel, hurdles and fencing. However, the myth dies hard even in these enlightened times.

In the seventeenth century the Weald witnessed quite a different change, this time in ideas, and great interest was aroused in the science of arboriculture and in the replanting of woodland with different trees. The man who did the arousing was John Evelyn through a single book written in 1664 called simply *Sylva*. He was to be the originator of the many beautiful wooded parklands so common throughout the south of England and the Weald generally; and ringed around Ashdown Forest today are Kidbrooke, Pippingford, Buckhurst, Eridge, Buxted and Sheffield Parks, which still survive as lasting memorials to an early conservationist.

The Weald was now planted with new species of trees such as

the silver fir (1607), and the European larch (1620), and increasingly with others that had long been there, but had grown almost unnoticed, like Norway spruce, sycamore and the native Scots pine. Another was that ancient, strange and slightly mysterious tree the hornbeam, which began to be coppiced and planted in hedgerows, especially in Sussex.

Here let us pause and consider instead the history of wildlife in the Wealden Forest.

The wolf has a long record of preying on man and beast alike, and in prehistoric times the Iron Age fortified mining camp on Saxonbury Hill, south of Frant, was as much for protection against wolves as human attack. Much later, in 731, the Venerable Bede refers to the Saxon Andredsweald as a place where 'wild boars were plentiful . . . and wolves preyed upon . . . deer'. The large Saxon herds must have been a great temptation for them. Place-names sometimes confirm this: for example, Woolpack Farm, in Bell Lane south of Nutley, which is from the Old English Wulfpyte—Wolves' Snare (eighth century). The name Boarzell, east of Ticehurst, comes from the Old English Bar(a)gesell, meaning a herdsman's camp where the boars stand.

Neither of these animals survived beyond the seventeenth century, but that did not stop the persistence of some extraordinary animal legends, like the St Leonard's Forest dragon or serpent of August 1614. An old printed document in the British Museum describes a 'loathly worm' 9 feet long shaped like the axle tree of a cart with black scales. It was stated to have killed two people and two dogs, 'being poysoned and very much swell, but not prayed upon'. Moreover there were several witnesses to all this. This is not nearly so far-fetched as it sounds. Only recently has anyone known about the Komodo Dragon, a huge reptile that lives on an Indonesian island. A bite from this animal is poisonous and fatal because it lives off carrion. Perhaps the 'loathly worm' was of a similar species?

Centuries earlier there had been the legend of St Leonard himself, whose fight with dragon had spilled its blood, and from the drops lilies-of-the-valley grew, as they do there today. Later, smugglers used these and other tales to stop people from prying on their routes through the still densely forested lands.

A nineteenth-century animal story from the same area is

rather more authentic, for in the Tilgate stone in the Wadhurst Clay Dr Gideon Mantell first discovered the fossil of the great herbivorous dinosaur, the iguanodon, an animal that had browsed along the shores of the freshwater Wealden delta some 150 million years ago.

To bring us into the twentieth century is a story from Donald Maxwell, that fine Sussex writer, who whilst exploring the Upper Medway near Fen Place Ponds, north of Turners Hill, met some children who told him about a horrific (but true) encounter with what they called a 'water boar'. They had run for their lives, and told local people, although they were disbelieved at first. At length a hunt was organized and an enormous wild boar shot which had escaped from an enclosure in the woods some years before and had been living in the wild area near the ponds (this area is in fact still something of a 'wildwood', as I discovered when researching for my book *Portrait of the River Medway*). However, anyone who has ever seen wild boar in a forest does not take them lightly; on one occasion when my wife and I were walking in the forests of the Belgian Ardennes we heard a tremendous thundering noise—and lo and behold! a large boar with several young rushed past shaking the very ground under our feet.

Naturally, this great forest was a haunt of bird life—the high canopy of trees, undergrowth, and ground layer providing an immense variety of habitats—but the record is scanty, although at one time there must have been many larger birds such as birds of prey. However, once again place-names provide a clue: Ramslye, near Frant, comes from *Hroefn* (raven) in 1262, and Eridge from eagle's ridge and *Earn* (eagle) in 1203. The last eagle in the Forest was not caught until 1834; ravens have often been introduced, as at Pippingford on Ashdown Forest, but they seem to prefer a more isolated or mountainous habitat.

Coming back to the seventeenth century and John Evelyn, whose original concern over the preservation of oaks had been for timber for the Navy, there is another legend that requires explaining. Much jolly stuff has been written about 'Hearts of Oak' and the 'Sussex Weed', but in reality my Lords at the Admiralty were more discerning and as Pepys noted in his diary: 'Prussian or Baltic oak was to be preferred'; this was because of its greater water-resistant quality. However, such oak was not easy to obtain, so the Admiralty had often to make do with Wealden oak instead.

During the eighteenth century the Wealden landscape had a 'new look' brought about by a vast increase in enclosures and the rise of the great landscape gardeners. The new enclosures, especially after 1750, needed many miles of new hedges for boundaries and along the turnpike roads, so there was an enormous demand for hedgerow trees like ash, hornbeam and elm, the last being a newcomer and advocated by a landscaper called Batty Langley. There were two other famous landscapers, Capability Brown, who laid out Sheffield Park, and Humphrey Repton, who organized the gardens at Kidbrooke Park, Forest Row, and Buckhurst Park at Withyham. It was Repton who once remarked on the treegrowing qualities of the Weald Clay: 'Every plant a bush, and every bush a tree'.

However, within the higher centre of the Weald the oak and beech woodlands appeared much the same as they had done for centuries. The oakwoods of course had been used as a crop, having been felled and replanted many times with coppicing and pollarding as normal practice. The really old oaks we can see now are almost always pollarded, such as the very fine specimens in Balcombe Forest on the western fringes of Ashdown, and some in Sheffield Park. If they are 39 to 43 feet in girth, they can be as much as 800 years old, whereas old oaks that are unpollarded are rarely more than 400 years of age.

Another change in the landscape was probably more than welcome. This was the coming of the turnpike roads. For centuries most Wealden roads had spent most of even a normal year looking like an unpaved farm track today in late autumn— a river of mud. The first turnpike in Sussex was from Godstone to East Grinstead in 1724, which reached Uckfield in 1752, and in 1754 arrived at the coast at Eastbourne. In due course this highway became the main London road, the modern A22, whose heavy traffic on occasions threatens the peace and quiet of Ashdown Forest.

But the dreadful Wealden roads did not worry the 'free traders', or smugglers, whose activities reached their peak in mid-century. Theirs was a major industry involving squire, parson, burgher and countryman; it was highly organized and professional, but its operators were exceedingly ferocious if interfered with. However, more of this anon, when we come to look at Ashdown Forest in detail.

With the increased enclosures came the wind of change in the farming world, following the work of the great improvers, like the seed drill of Jethro Tull and crop rotation of Coke of Holkham, which were seen and recorded by Arthur Young, the best agricultural reporter Britain has ever had. However, when he came to the Weald, particularly Sussex, he disapproved of the landlords and their woodlands. Young thought that the old traditional wooded shaws and hedgerows cut out the light from the growing corn. We can pause here and consider the loss of our hedgerows today, when highly mechanized farming demands endless and rather soulless prairies of wheat and barley; but Young was travelling through an England far less crowded and urbanized, and probably greener than today. Even well into the nineteenth century Sussex was very much sunk into its land-scape, its local life had hardly changed for centuries, and it was picturesque and difficult to cross with its wooded ridges, deep vales and sticky claylands.

But the agricultural revolution which had brought to Sussex by 1840 (the year that chemical fertilizers were introduced) the greatest extent ever of its arable land and which was to reach its zenith with Victorian High Farming in mid-century, also had its darker side. In the years following 1820 the Weald was the most agriculturally depressed region in Britain and a report in 1833 said there was scarcely a solvent tenant farmer in the Weald. In 1830 the lot of the landless labourer was worse than it had ever been since the Norman Conquest. Both Arthur Young and William Cobbett had said if there was no improvement in rural conditions, Britain would see a repeat of the French Revolution. This social upheaval did not take place, but instead came a religious revival—which perhaps prevented an English Reign of Terror—and the still heavily forested Weald remained serene and tranquil throughout the century. Later it became criss-crossed with branch railways, which probably improved life and ended the harsher aspects of isolation. In about 1860 an interesting development that could be seen on many farms in East Sussex was the growing of hops, together with a carefully calculated area of woodland, usually ash trees, for the poles.

However, throughout the area of the old Wealden Forest little real forestry was practised and by 1900 much of the existing woodland was in poor condition, except on some of the larger private estates. The late eighteenth-century enthusiasm for landscape and agriculture caused interest in forestry to wane, a state from which England has not really recovered, for as foresters we are sadly behind most European nations. An improvement came in the years just before the First World War with the introduction of chestnut coppicing to make straight wood palings for a growing market, but was soon overshadowed by the war. This brought a dreadful drain on Wealden timber, and many trees ended their days propping up trenches or making duckboards in the mud and blood of the Somme and Passchendaele.

In 1919 the Forestry Commission was formed to try and reduce the vast imports of soft timber, and sheer economic necessity meant planting fast-growing conifers like the Sitka spruce and Douglas fir. In places of poor soil and where hard-woods would not flourish they planted Western Red Cedar and Hemlock. Some were planted at Challock in East Kent and over in the western Weald on the heavy Weald clay; another small plantation is Furnace Wood on the southern borders of Ashdown Forest. At Bedgebury in the High Weald, south of Goudhurst, in the National Pinetum which besides its many species of conifers also has some rare oaks and maple trees.

The Commission has been harshly criticized for its conifers— and perhaps in the better climate of the 1920s more hardwoods should have been planted—but much of the criticism has been emotional rather than practical. Some of it has been sheer nonsense, like the notion that conifer woods contain no wildlife. Norway spruce, for example, provides a home for the smallest British bird, the Goldcrest, as well as for wrens, chaffinches and coal tits, not to mention the odd heronry as well. This view is also amply borne out on Ashdown Forest itself where some of the larger private enclosed estates have quite sizeable conifer plantations or groups, such as at Pippingford Park and Old Lodge, where Douglas fir and Scots pines seem to have plenty of bird and animal life.

Between the two world wars the Wealden woods were better maintained than they had been for many years; their relative isolation was a walker's paradise for often you could get to them only by branch-line railways, the expensive motor car being just a dot on the horizon.

The 1939–45 war brought further inroads on Wealden timber, but at least out of it came planning legislation to protect the remaining hardwoods. Unfortunately nobody realized, least of all the planners, what the great social revolution of the welfare state, and increased mobility of the consumer society that followed it, would bring in its wake with the metropolitan invasion increasing and the dormitory towns expanding. The sheer weight of numbers of everything, whether it has been population increase, suburbia, cars, litter, and then out in the country pesticides, motorized farmers and—perhaps worst of all—noise, has imposed a very heavy strain on the best hardwood forest landscape in Britain. Nevertheless, out of this technological and materialistic mania at least has come a realization of the urgency to protect the woodland environment and its ecology before it is too late. Even as I write seismic tests of a positive nature within the rocks of the High Weald have been announced at Horsted Keynes and Crowborough in the greedy quest for oil and natural gas, and with Ashdown Forest lying in between there must be many fears regarding its future as a surviving wilderness.

However, the Weald is still the most forested part of Britain, and Sussex the most wooded county with the High Weald having the best hardwoods in the land. But it must always be realized that this beautiful wooded landscape of the Forest Ridges is in reality a managed one, even though some centuries passed in the making of it, and only Ashdown Forest is in any way an extensive relic of the once huge wildwood that stretched for over a hundred miles across the south of England from the Hampshire Downs to East Kent.

We are now at the end of this brief glimpse at the history of the Wealden Forest, and imagination must picture the Roman legionary looking out over his Silva Anderida and his successor, the Saxon pioneer farmer, seeing the great Andredsweald spreading out before him.

Perhaps one can go a little closer to this vision by standing on one of Ashdown's crests on a clear bright day and staring hard into the blue distance, where the all-embracing view of isolated trees, coppices, clumps, copses and shaws will all blur into an impression of unbroken forest. For a fleeting moment the eye will see a wilderness, the millennium of Man's impact fades away, and the Wealden Forest is seen as the Old Stone Age hunters saw it.

2

The Northern Slopes of Ashdown Forest

The heart of this book is Ashdown Forest's open heights, but the Forest was very much larger many centuries ago, and always in the background, like some folk memory, is the once great forest of the Weald. To trace Ashdown's story it is necessary to travel well beyond the present borders, which have been fixed twice in its history: in the fourteenth century by the Crown, and in the seventeenth century by a legal document.

The northern slopes and fringes of Ashdown contain most of the upper basin of the River Medway. This basin is a large half-saucer of country that stretches from Lingfield in Surrey, through Turners Hill in West Sussex, across Ashdown Forest, over Crowborough Beacon and Saxonbury Hill in East Sussex to Tunbridge Wells and Tonbridge in Kent.

We are not concerned here with the outer ramparts, but what lies between is a large part of the central High Weald, and into the northern slopes of Ashdown merge imperceptibly. In early medieval times, in fact, the northern boundary of the Forest was the River Medway.

The journey can begin in the woods around Gravetye Manor, where on one of the higher dry gravelly terraces of a Medway headwater lies the beautiful Elizabethan mansion of Gravetye built in 1598 by Richard Infield, a prosperous ironmaster; today it is a hotel and country club, and a member of the International Relais and Châteaux organization, with the surroundings of a lake renowned for trout fishing and gardens that became famous for their revolutionary breakaway from Victorian bedding plants through a great gardener, William Robinson.

The woods, some of whose oaks may well be a surviving fragment of the primeval forest, are now the property of the Forestry Commission and are interlaced with footpaths and bridleways. One of these will at length bring the walker to Weir Wood Reservoir where our exploratory journey can divide north and south of this sheet of water. These routes largely follow the Medway valley, but here we are more concerned with the influences of the Forest than with those of the river.

Northwards of Willets Bridge at the western end of Weir Wood are the impressive tree-covered sandstone crags of Stone Farm Rocks, popular with aspiring climbers. Here they are festooned with oaks, yews, Scots pines and holly trees. The holly is often an understorey tree in oak and beechwoods, but the yew, one of Britain's three native conifers, appears to grow almost anywhere, indifferent to soil.

Further along the East Grinstead road is Saint Hill Green with more crags. The name has nothing holy in its origin, but is a faint reminder of the early pioneers clearing the forest by fire, for it comes from the O.E. *saenget*, which meant burnt clearing. Its Germanic roots are seen today in the place called Sengel in Westphalia, meaning the same thing.

Soon the ever-spreading suburbs of East Grinstead appear, which now hide an old market town with a fine High Street and some good timber-framed buildings like Clarendon House. It began as a forest clearing, hence the name—Greenstede or green place—and grew into a borough with two M.P.s, became an important assize town, and was the nearest market town to the Forest, which lay astride its routes to the south and south-east. The first turnpike road came to the town in 1724, and was later extended across Ashdown in mid-century; but the town may have been unpopular with certain forest dwellers for many smugglers, highwaymen and petty thieves were tried there. About this time it even had a theatre, but the performances were sometimes interrupted, for a playbill of May 1758 reads: 'The great yard dog that made so much noise on Thursday night during the last act of King Richard the Third will be sent to a neighbour's over the way.' Cobbett does not seem to have liked the town any more than he did Ashdown Forest, for he described it in January 1822 thus: '. . . a rotten borough and a very shabby place'.

'Right against the forest fence, by St Agnes' fountain.' This line from the carol 'Good King Wenceslas', by John Mason Neale, written in 1849 when he was Warden of Sackville College (the fine Jacobean Almshouses in East Grinstead), is thought to have come from Neale's association with Ashdown Forest.

The railway reached the town in 1855, and with later a station at Forest Row, the outskirts of the Forest were within a comfortable carriage ride—if you had one—and some of its isolation was broken down.

Towards the close of the nineteenth century East Grinstead was at the eastern end of the developing High Weald from Horsham, and saw the building of many villas in vastly varied styles. All this seems to have receded by 1939, and Sir Osbert Sitwell described it as the 'sunset hour of one of the periodic calms in history'. However, since the end of the war the calm has gone and been replaced by a frenzied rash of expensive brick boxes to house commuters.

Just south of the town is Ashurstwood, really a suburb now. The most interesting place there is Grantham's forge with its high-quality ironwork.

Eastwards from the high ground around the town is a pleasantly remote rural green area between the busy A264 and the Medway valley route which can be reached from the main A22 south of the town by a bridleway to Shovelstrode Farm. The name here means marshy ground by the slope, which seems right enough, for the small Cansiron stream flows out of the boggy ground not far away to join the Medway. The farm itself, a beautiful building with shaved lawns, I found hard to believe was a real farm.

From here by wooded footpaths, most of which are in a very poor state, you can reach the main Tunbridge Wells road (A264), and make a worthwhile little diversion. For along a side road northwards and over the Kent Water stream, and just inside Surrey, you might like to peep at Lullenden, a low grey stone Wealden house. This was where the Churchills lived from 1917 to 1919, presided over, so they said, by a 'tyrant of a gardener and bailiff'.

Back along the main road still in wooded country appears Hammerwood. At first it seems that there is only a large church standing in splendid isolation just off the road. But retreat a few hundred yards, and down a lane will be a few surprises. However, before doing that take a walk around the church, St Stephen's, which is just over a hundred years old and a fine building which may represent the social phenomenon of the growth of Victorian villadom we touched on a while back. The prospect southwards from the rear is very fine for there is a good view of distant Ashdown and in between the typical Wealden ridge and valley landscape, and looking across one can recall an image of long past Saxon Andredsweald.

Down the lane, which at first appears a little cluttered with odd parked cars like stranded whales, there are some very interesting houses. First there are two close together: the Tudor Bower Farmhouse with studded timberwork (that is, the vertical members of a timber-framed wall) and a Horsham slabbed stone roof, and inside a 1595 fireplace and a very tall newel post (that is, the post at the stairhead which supports the hand rails); this one is the full height of the house. The second building, Hammerwood, is quite different, being one of Norman Shaw's very large and comfortable 'Old English' designs built in 1872 with some high Tudor chimneys.

Then right down the bottom of the lane towards the marshy valley of the little Cansiron stream, with a very fine view once again towards Ashdown, is a house whose architect and whose history deserve much more space than I can give and which recently has taken an exciting new turn.

The architect was Benjamin Latrobe, born in 1764 in Yorkshire, but educated in Saxony, and influenced by the French architect Claude-Nicholas Ledoux who built for Louis XVI. Latrobe was a truly remarkable man, for he was also a fine engineer who studied under Smeaton, the builder of the Eddystone Lighthouse. Except for the two houses built in Sussex, after 1796 all his work was carried out in the young United States, where he became the first professional architect, and adviser to President Jefferson. His achievements included Baltimore Cathedral and Exchange, the Bank of Philadelphia and the University of Virginia. His engineering skill brought even greater rewards, for he built the first American city water

supply in Philadelphia and others in New Orleans and
Pennsylvania State. These were the exciting early days of
steam, and Latrobe's talents produced steamboats on the Ohio
River and steam power for textile factories.

His first and best English work is Hammerwood Park—the
other, Ashdown House, is two miles further south, which we
shall see on our southern journey. He was a pioneer of the Greek
revival, and Hammerwood Park, built in ashlar-dressed stone,
reflects this new approach to the Classic style with the complete
symmetry of its southern façade. This has three bays, in the
centre giant Doric pilasters flanked by two Doric porticos; on the
West portico is a Greek inscription which reads: 'Of John
Spurling's mansion, the architect B. H. Latrobe made the first
portico in 1792 AD and the second year of the 642nd Olympiad.'
Architects evidently knew their classical history then, a trend
that continued well into the Railway Age, and then sadly
disappeared.

Spurling did not have his house long; and in 1880 it became
the property of Oswald Augustus Smith and entered on a period
when it must have been a very pleasant place to live in—at least
for children, for a poem written about 1905–10 runs:

> There is a house that stands four square, to meet the sun all day,
> And those who come to visit there, forget to go away,
> It's full of toys and girls and boys, and all of them are good,
> And fun and games go on all day, at happy Hammerwood.

Its later modern history is less happy, for its interior was
almost wrecked by conversion into eleven flats, and then a Pop
group called the Zeppelins bought it. Evidently, they had not
thought about its acoustics or the aircraft noise which is a
feature of the area, for they made only one recording here, and
then went off to America and forgot about it.

And there it stood empty and forlorn until 1982, when a
remarkable young man called David Pinegar decided it was
worth saving this unusually fine house and bought it to restore.
I had the pleasure of meeting him and hearing about the
exciting plans he has to restore the building and open it for the
public at certain times for musical recitals of the lesser-known
composers and to commemorate certain historical events. His
greatest problem has been dry rot, which was unfortunately

hidden by the conversion to flats, and which the Department of the Environment grant does not cover.

I was shown over the empty shell of the house with its superb oak galleried staircase, spacious rooms—even the servants' quarters had plenty of space—and had revealed to me a number of architectural niceties. One was the splendid Venetian double arch window, the forerunner for the Senate at the Washington Capitol which Latrobe restored after the British had burnt it in 1814. Another item was a large fireplace with the Sun King's insignia, made by a London firm. And then there were the Coade stone floral decoration (fleur de lys and rose) under the Doric cornices; this is a fired ceramic—the same reconstituted material that Nash used for the caryatids on his famous terraces. This material has a curious, almost romantic, history for it was produced by a Miss Coade, who employed Italian craftsmen; but after some amorous overtures she sacked them and the firm ended abruptly, the secret dying with her.

Outside is an example of Latrobe's water engineering and drainage skills in the way he controlled the spring line all round Hammerwood to feed a tank for the house water supply.

After all this one must await with great interest the day when the house opens once more as a fully restored building.

The name Hammerwood recalls ironworking, which was both Roman and Tudor in the Cansiron area; the more recent discoveries of Roman ironworking and a pottery kiln will be described in Chapter 9.

Here we are on an outcrop of the Ashdown Beds, and further along at Holtye Common—the name means Hollow Place—the sandy sterile nature of the ground is shown by a stretch of heathland, a veritable Ashdown Forest in miniature. Past Holtye and up and down along the ridge the hamlet of Blackham appears, its name meaning simply Black Enclosure, a clearing by fire perhaps? Anyhow, the black now is from its constant roaring traffic exhausts, and it is hard to believe that it was a very rural spot before the war. The community is centred round the Sussex Oak Inn on the main road, above which ran the old coach road. Older people I talked to remembered bare knuckle fighting taking place behind the inn. Holywich Wood just to the north had a flourishing charcoal-burning trade, and in the severe winter of 1927 there was skating on the lake in the grounds of Highfields, the 'big house' down the lane southwards, once owned by Lord Maugham, the brother of the famous Somerset, the novelist.

The most interesting house here is Blackham Court, a Wealden building overlooking the Medway valley and a kind of manor house at one time, for behind it is a moat. This was probably a fish stew fed by a tiny tributary of the main river which turns north at this point. These Wealden moated houses in Kent and Sussex probably acquired the custom of keeping fish from the earlier monastic houses to vary the winter salt meat diet as well as for holy fast days. The moat here encircles a mound which is now a tennis court, but the site was at one time a very large building.

From Blackham we come down into Kent at the small village of Ashurst on the Medway by the railway, which arrived in 1888, and thankfully is still here. The place is small, under two hundred people—also thankfully—and the church, St Martin of Tours of tenth-century foundation, is just up the hill and off the main road. It had a fifteenth-century tower during the Wealden cloth trade revival, when surplus cash was available to build it. Inside is a memorial to Elias Allen, a native of the village (158?–1654) who was the greatest mathematical instrument maker of his day and made a Universal Dial or Circumferator. This was a surveying instrument which used a magnetic needle swinging round a dial mounted on a tripod. In the porch is a Wealden ironworks panel, for this small place was once quite a large ironworking centre. Later when I was wandering round one of the cornfields near the river I found iron slag amongst the stubble, grubbed up by ploughing.

Ashurst used to have a large water mill and one of its white weather-boarded buildings, which is still in good condition, has a surprise, for it is the home of a thriving frozen seafoods business. Far it seems from the sea, and even further from the source of its raw material—prime Norwegian prawns from Alesund in north-west Norway. The company, which is small but with a large turnover, employs local people, and I was shown over this highly efficient little plant hidden behind white wooden walls by one of the directors, Roger Smith, an ex-fishing skipper from Newhaven. He was revealing about his former profession, saying it was almost totally unreliable, as often when conditions were good (perhaps when a large shoal was sighted) the crew were often absent or simply would not put out to sea. Which is fish food for thought, especially when you hear of British fishermen complaining about fishing grounds and their limits.

Outside the building where the old mill leat ran is now almost a kind of water garden with runner beans alongside Himalayan balsam, a widespread river plant nowadays, and a fine large Douglas fir—all making a pleasant if strange sight.

From Ashurst we move gently towards Tunbridge Wells, not by the noisy A264, either down a lane or by the many footpaths to Old Groombridge, as opposed to the largely Victorian Sussex village. Groombridge in the eighteenth century was a centre of smuggling with a ferocious gang, which sold 300 pounds of tea a week, and its leader, Bowra, built a large house here from the profits; but I have never been able to find it.

We move up past the attractive triangular green with the popular Crown Inn, and on up the hill until the right is a row of tall terraced cottages in local sandstone with slate roof dormers, originally thatched, the whole compact group being about 150 years old. I suppose I must have passed them well over a hundred times and they have always interested me, and so one Sunday I stopped and asked an inhabitant, Mr Edwards, working in his garden to tell me about them. He was a cheerful conversationalist, and said they were estate cottages for Top Hill Farm, which borders Groombridge Place. He was a Surrey man, who remembers spending much of his boyhood wandering in Hampton Court Park after crossing the Thames by a penny ferry, and mused on what Charles II would think of the traffic now on the hill he used to ride slowly up after his stay at Groombridge Place.

From here, to avoid the tedious outer suburbs of Tunbridge Wells, which seem to have swamped the village of Langton Green, it is better to go down the lane towards the Hungershall stream, or River Groom, and the railway and then along to High Rocks, and its pub.

This was an old coaching inn, and according to an ex-farmer I met called Fred, it had been in the very recent past a great meeting-place for many actors, singers and people of the entertainment world like Miles Malleson of Glyndebourne and Jack

Payne, as well as statesmen like Lord Hailsham, Lord Soames and many foreign ambassadors whose Rolls were lined along the path outside. He said it was due to an extremely enterprising landlord, but after his demise those that followed had made structural alterations and lost the rather jolly atmosphere the inn had once had.

Opposite the inn are some old stables which have now been refurbished into tearooms, and they look very elegant indeed and quite fit their surroundings. The High Rocks themselves belong to the inn, and outside is a small well-worn notice: 'Never to be said unto your shame, that all was beauty till here you came'—trite, but rather more necessary now than one would wish.

The rocks are high crags of Ardingly sandstone from the Tunbridge Wells Sands of Cretaceous Age, and were formed under the very severe conditions of the Tundra climates that existed in the various Ice Ages when all north of the Thames was ice. They are very popular with budding climbers, who seem to be younger than ever, and are highly expert with their sophisticated equipment.

After this we climb up the steep Teagarden Lane, where there are exceptionally fine views over the hilly wooded landscape, and not only are you reminded of the Wealden Forest again, but also that until well into the seventeenth century there was little else but trees between here and Ashdown Forest.

Into the old spa town, which in spite of being one of the most overcrowded places that I know, has still a great deal of charm in its commons and the eighteenth-century Pantiles to recall a more elegant era.

We return now eastwards to the shores of Weir Wood, and start our southerly journey. The lake, if I can call it so, is now a good habitat for waterfowl. On a fine sunny clear day in late March I noticed, not without help from the more expert bird watchers, that besides the fairly common Great Crested Grebe, Barnacle and Canada Geese, Common Mallard and Shelduck were also a Goldeye (a winter migrant) and the rare Red Crested Pochard which I was told was an 'escape'. From here eastwards it is difficult to pass by the lake shore, for it is very private, but by taking footpaths and going via Mudbrooks Farm—now a Wildfowl Park called Springhill—and skirting the edge of the

Forest you can reach the road to Forest Row.

Along here on the very edge of Ashdown Forest there is a house named Wretham Lodge, built in 1912, and the home of a very enterprising lady called Anne Lumsden. She farms locally, and is an elected Commoner on the Board of Conservators of Ashdown Forest, so talking to her was both interesting and informative.

She runs eighty sheep and breeds Welsh ponies on land adjoining, but not on, the Forest, where she had at one time grazed sheep; but alas no longer, for the hazards of stock on the Forest these days with heavy traffic, careless drivers and un-fenced roads are too great. However, as she pointed out—and I was to hear this said very often in and around the Forest—if people want the open character of the Forest to stay, then grazing stock on it is the only answer; but perhaps under different conditions to those at present. Anne Lumsden was born and bred on the Forest and at one time, before it was flooded, farmed land in the Weir Wood valley. This was originally at a low rent, but Horsham Water Board thought she got it too cheaply and raised the rent by 500 per cent however, as she said, not all the land was good, some of it being decidedly swampy and not very useful for grazing sheep. In 1976 the level of the reservoir fell so low during the long hot dry summer that the old Admiral's bridge was once more in daylight. The name here is thought to refer to the Tudor Lord Admiral Seymour, a personage we shall come across later, but in rather a different way.

Her final remark intrigued me: she said that Forest Row's name was derived from the French Forêt du Roi, which then became Foreign Row and finally corrupted into Forest Row. This is not the normally accepted derivation, but it sounded authentic enough to me with the long usage of Norman French lasting into the time when Ashdown became a Royal Forest.

A more interesting way into Forest Row is by a bridleway that leads past the forlorn 300-year-old ruin of Brambletye House, a Jacobean building whose last tenant, Sir James Richards—who had a Spanish wife, Beatriz Ferrara—fled to Spain suspected of treason, where later his descendants became famous Spanish generals. The estate has had many owners since, and the present owner of Brambletye Manor Farm is Michael Dunn,

recently arrived from a very different part of the world—
Northumberland, where he farmed 350 acres on Coal Measure
soils under the constant threat of open-cast mining. I found him
a quiet practical man intrigued by his greener and damper
surroundings after the cold, dry open climate of the north-east.
He has inherited an ancient moated site and a semi-ruined
traditional Sussex barn which, as he told me, he would like to
repair, but it would almost ruin him to do so . . . sic transit gloria
Sussexensis!

And so to Forest Row, nowadays for me a disappointing sort of
place with its noisy main road and suburban growth despite the
elegance of Ryst and Forest Roads and the 1452 Chequers Inn.
Walhill Farm on the north side of the infant Medway recalls the
older name of the original hamlet: Walhatch, and Walhillhatch
the medieval entrance to a larger Ashdown than now. Its most
famous modern inhabitant could well be Mr Michael Quinn, the
chef at the Ritz in London.

Eastwards along the road from Forest Row are some scattered
Ashdown Forest fringe settlements like Quabrook, Parrock and
Coleman's Hatch; the latter, although old, has a fine modern
church built in 1913 in Early English style.

North of Forest Row are two places, Pixton Hill and Pock Hill,
whose names are rather mysterious, for they both refer to pixies
or fairies—from Puck, O.E. *puca*, an evil or mischievous
demon—and gave Rudyard Kipling the idea of *Puck of Pook's
Hill*.

Going south and east again, still on the north bank of the
river, Ashdown House School comes into view; Latrobe's second
house forms part of the buildings grouped here. It has been
described as a feminine version of Hammerwood Park's main
block, but the outside is generally plain except where the eye is
drawn to the circular porch with four elegant Ionic columns.

The boys' school was founded in 1886 by two brothers from
Brighton, and was built up round the core of a Tudor stone
farmhouse and Latrobe's Classical house with classrooms added
in 1934. Mrs Hill, now living in Nutley on Ashdown Forest, can
remember being in service here in 1912; it has now become a
famous co-educational preparatory school

Further along is Parrock, a very pleasant spot, where in the
middle of July I camped by a field of dredge corn (barley and

wheat mixed). And all was very peaceful except for the aircraft and distant whirr of grass driers. Later on I walked down to the river, which is very weedy just here, and I thought it was easy enough to visualize the Forest once reaching down to the marshy flood plain. There was a faint drowsy whirring along the river where dragonflies and some rather rarer damsel flies (*Agrion virgo splendens*) were catching the sunlight with their wings, the females' transparent and the males' a dazzling blue. Over the river by a gate I watched some sheep drinking out of buckets, and on the way back I passed Forest Row's sewage plant, neat but noxious. The only disturbing thought was why in this rather rural area are some of the inhabitants so bent on continually modernizing their houses and barns—are they really farmers, and is there really an economic crisis?

Soon along here we are in Hartfield, a typical Ashdown fringe village comfortably sited on a Medway terrace fifty feet above the valley, away from flood dangers. It was carved out of the Wealden Forest, and its name comes from the subsequent grazing of deer there. Much later the village was involved with smuggling, and the much-restored and attractive pub called The Gallipot Inn at Upper Hartfield was once their haunt. In another, the Hay Waggon, I had a long lunch-time chat with two locals. One was retired and running sheep as a hobby, the other (I suppose inadvertently appropriate) was a local butcher! However, it is from such conversations that one finds the thread of life in a community. One topic thus was the closure of the local Craft Centre; it would appear that these kind of enterprises are often artificial in England—a country far too urbanized, and with too long an industrial history, and where real rural artisan work has long since disappeared. One must go deep into the Ardennes or rural France to see it genuinely active.

Hartfield lost one of its old sixteenth-century farmhouses by fire in 1982, North Clays in Butcherfield Lane, whilst it was empty—the fire risk with these splendid old buildings is always present.

From Hartfield it is but a step along the highroad to another Forest village—Withyham—a charming place with a fine old Georgian pub, the Dorset Arms, a white weather-boarded building with decorated barge-boards of the early nineteenth century (i.e. boards which project against the slope of the gable).

It is quite hard today in the still peaceful atmosphere of this small village to visualize the darker side of rural poverty in the villages around Ashdown Forest in 1830. On 15th October in that year a mob of some 300 farmworkers from Rotherfield marched into Withyham chanting for parsons to lower their tithes and farmers to raise their wages. They were met by the Earl de la Warr's steward, and at length dispersed, but in their bitterness they called the Withyham labourers a 'set of cowards' for not standing up for their rights. Perhaps the Withyham men were content with their lot or perhaps they feared their masters. This area had many large estates, and one right opposite here is Buckhurst Park, which stretches up to, and includes, land within the Forest with today many footpaths through it to Ashdown. The name Buckhurst means 'Beechwood Hill', and as most of the estate is on Ashdown sands, and the remainder on Ardingly sandstone, we can imagine a great sweep of beech-woods on this free-draining soil from the Forest right down to the Medway.

Here has been the family home of the Sackvilles since the thirteenth century, when Jordan de Sackville married Ela Dene, the heiress of the family which owned Buckhurst Park. They are an extremely ancient family of Norman and pre-viously Danish origin who became large landowners in Sussex and prospered, Elizabeth I raising her Lord Treasurer, Thomas Sackville, to the peerage, and granting him Knole at Sevenoaks—the large and magnificent former Archbishop's Palace. Incidentally, Thomas was no mean poet and playwright, who gave England its first classic tragedy, *Gorboduc*. They were made Earls of Dorset by James I and Dukes by George II, and after the 5th Duke, the line became Earls de la Warr (West).

The family home remains, but the original house, Old Buckhurst, decayed after the move to Knole, which was then far more convenient, and stone was taken to build Sackville College at East Grinstead. The newer house, Buckhurst Park, arose out of the old hunting lodge in 1690, and its present large ornamental lake was the furnace pond of the Stoneland furnace and forge worked by Sir John Baker of Mayfield. Stonelands was for some time a separate park from Buckhurst. The family have had a very long and not always harmonious association with the Commoners of Ashdown Forest, but the present Earl de la Warr as Lord of the Manor of Duddleswell is represented on the Board of Conservators there, and co-operation is maintained.

Before leaving Withyham a visit to the church is interesting because it is virtually a Sackville shrine, and one can see there a Doom, that is a painting of the Last Judgement, by the Reverend Earl de la Warr in 1841, an early Victorian rector who made Withyham the first church to follow Cardinal Newman's Oxford Movement. The Rectory has an interesting verandah in front, but the pride of the village is surely Duckings, a very fine Wealden house opposite the road to Balls Green. Built by John Baker of Mayfield, father of Sir John, both ironmasters, the house passed in 1570 to the Sackvilles, but from 1684 to 1910 the house and farm were leased to the Hall family, which is considered to be the longest lease ever held in England. After this the gardens were laid out by Mr and Mrs Clement Weir with particular care and Richard Jeffreys described the house as being one a man could not tear himself away from. I was extremely lucky to see the garden and outside of the house, after having been cautiously but kindly invited in by the present owner.

After Duckings you can take a side road and approach the cross-roads south-west of Cherrygardens Farm, where you can pick fruit in season or excellent vegetables, including aubergines.

We are now in Ardingly sandstone country where massive crags outcrop in the grounds of several large houses, and some have been landscaped in a very attractive way over the years. Penns-in-the-Rocks, once the home of my distant ancestor William Penn, standing in an 1,800-acre wooded estate, is one of these houses. The approach is through the steep valley of the small Motts Mill stream, and the actual rock-girt site could well be prehistoric; archaeological work is going on at present within the grounds.

The house itself was once called Rocks Farm and enlarged and given in the 1730s a fine Georgian south front with a doorway having alternate stone quoin blocks, and a century later pretty well rebuilt to make a comfortable family residence. It has had a long list of tenants and owners, some mysterious, after William Penn IV (Penn's grandson) had altered it, and between the wars a poetess, Dorothy Wellesley, lived there. Lord Gibson has

owned the house since 1958, after having completely refurbished it in 1957–9, and through his kindness I was able to be
shown over it by his knowledgeable butler, Michael Green-
berry, one-time sergeant in the Grenadier Guards.

Inside is delightful and all in good taste; the small Jewel or
Gem Room (once the old hall) has a large Charles II fireback,
appropriate enough for iron may well have been worked in the
grounds in Roman or Tudor times—at present there is no
evidence. The dining-room is intimate, with a ceiling that has
four 'porthole' mirrors at each corner, a fine effect and designed
by Lord Gibson. The fireplace has a portrait of the Iron Duke—
the Wellesley connection. Upstairs in Lady Gibson's room is a
fine four-poster of painted wood, and a superb painting, 'Shells
of the Ocean' by C. E. Hicks. The guest suite has a décor of a pink
flower-pattern raised linen walls and matching counterpanes—
not normally my colour, but here it is perfect. Amongst the
interesting objects the house possesses is a letter in the Hall
from General Napoleon, in the Year 4 (1795) on 20th
Vendémiaire addressed to M. Otto, an Austrian in the entour-
age of Emperor Franz II, the beginning of Napoleon's rise to
supreme power. Outside there was another large and heavy
fireback with the fleur-de-lys emblem, and it set me thinking
how such a heavy object came to be there.

The grounds contain a magnificent 300-year-old cedar, one of
the owner's favourite trees, and represents Lord Gibson's great
interest in forestry and as Chairman of the National Trust. A
footpath through the grounds leads to the narrow Motts Mill
valley, and there is a pleasant route to Eridge by way of a
curious hamlet called The Forstal. The name is common
enough, but has different meanings in Sussex, where it refers to
a stall in front of a farm, whilst in Kent it means a paddock near
a farmhouse.

From here we can have a look at The Warren, part of the old
Waterdowne Forest, now called Broadwater, and we are within
a remnant of the ancient Wealden Forest. It is made all the more
impressive by the spectacular Eridge Rocks, which are massive
crags of the now familiar Ardingly sandstone. One huge lump
called the Elephant Rock has great trees of beech, pines and
holly springing forth from its crevices and fissures. The rocks
are all weathered in a honeycomb fashion, and at length end

abruptly against one of the two largest geological faults in the central Weald. This is where the sandstone is thrust up against the Ashdown Beds along the line of the South Groombridge Fault.

Nearby are enormous rhododendrons and the whole assemblage of rocks, trees and plants makes for a wild natural landscape, and one can readily imagine primitive hunters seeking for a place to ambush or perhaps to shelter. In The Warren was found once the rare Spring Gentian (*Gentiana verna*), originally called the Felwort of the Spring—a bright-blue solitary flower.

From this wooded enclave midway between crowded Tunbridge Wells and open Ashdown we can cross the A26 road and walk through the spacious Eridge Park, the home of the Nevill family, Earls and Marquesses of Abergavenny, once known as Burgavenny.

This family in the later Middle Ages was not only the most powerful in Sussex, but also in the entire kingdom. Amongst them was the Earl of Warwick, the Kingmaker, at whose board it is said 30,000 people lived daily throughout the different castles and manors in England. He was the last of the great barons, feared even by the Crown, who made civil government all but impossible.

After all this, the history of the house here is rather modest, for although the family have been at Eridge since at least 1300, the earlier mansion was abandoned in the seventeenth century, probably due to a fire, and they went to Kidbrooke Park for a while before returning to Eridge in 1790. The restored house was made into a huge castellated Gothic pile and called Eridge Castle. This lasted until 1938, when the father of the present Marquess demolished it and built the present house on its site, and even this has been greatly reduced in size and is now known once again as Eridge Park.

To walk across this vast open park is an experience, and one has to realize that certainly up to about 1372 Waterdowne, Eridge and Rotherfield were all one great stretch of forest and deer park, reaching out to Ashdown Forest, then an unenclosed hunting ground. Much of the land here is now farmed with sheep, sown with wheat and colourful yellow rapeseed, and the large central lake, once a furnace pond, is now superbly ornamented with a long chain of pen ponds above the stream originally used for storing furnace and forge water. My wife and I walked through these fine grounds in late May along the footpath which passes through woods and crosses the stream where the forge was sited. The flowers were glorious, with buttercups and great sweeps of bluebells, particularly fine in 1982, amongst the magnificent beeches interspersed with the understorey trees of holly, and along the streams and ponds were masses of yellow flags. By the pen ponds we discovered the small field gentian, and away in the distant parkland were spread the fine oaks, and with the open breezy landscape the place was utterly unspoilt by houses, people or the eternal traffic.

There is another footpath further north that borders the deer park, but when I tried it later in the summer it was very cut up by horses—perhaps escaping from the noisy A26 as I was—but the rewards for struggling along the route in wellingtons were very fine trees and seeing the large herd of fallow deer at close quarters.

Both paths bring you to the still very pleasant village of Frant with its spacious green, which accords with the name, which is from the O.E. Fearn, fern- or bracken-covered place. The church of St Alban, although on an extremely ancient site—AD 700—was built in 1821, when the Hon. William Nevill was vicar, which somehow makes one immediately think of Jane Austen. However, it is a fine building, and interesting in that it was the only country church built in Sussex during that period; like Withyham it is associated with the local family, the Nevills, and inside has some notable features. The nave has four pillars of Sussex iron, with three graveslabs of 1631 and the chancel has work by a local wood carver, Frank Rosier, who died in 1946. There is a memorial to Colonel Buy, Royal Engineers, Frant's most famous native, who founded Ottawa—originally Bytown.

Outside in the village is Sternfold Park. The name here is an interesting example of derivation: originally Scearn-falod, dirty fold, then home of Roger de Sharnefold and later Sternfold, so the place is old even if the building is not. It is set in a close, described by a certain well-known archicologist—a word I have coined like musicologist, to mean one who describes buildings— as 'joyless, plain and Italianate'. But I thought it had a very fine façade, and from its site are magnificent views over the Weald, which were enhanced by the Scots pines in the grounds.

Down the Wadhurst Road is elegant Frant Place, once called Henley House and surrounded by magnificent grounds and gardens. It is now the Conference and Education Centre of the N.U.R.

From Frant we go once more to Tunbridge Wells by a completely forested approach, down the A267 and by a side road to the A26 and then to Strawberry Hill, and thus reach High Rocks by passing along near the ancient fort—covered in bluebells when I last saw it. This was discovered in 1939 by Mr J. H. Money and excavated in 1940 and again in 1957–61, which produced a varied collection of pottery, rings, footrings, bowls as well as hearths and flints, which has pushed back the date to nearly 5,000 years ago.

So with the forest reaching to their very door, here dwelt these prehistoric inhabitants of a primeval Tunbridge Wells long before Lord North stumbled on his iron spring whilst walking in the woods.

Finally, I once climbed on to the roof of a very tall house in Mount Sion and there before me beyond the roof tops not far off was a long line of trees stretching into the middle distance—my Wealden Forest was still there, if only as a re-created vision by height and distance lending enchantment.

3

The Eastern Ridges

The eastern edge of Ashdown Forest is high land, the highest point in fact of the High Weald, for Crowborough Beacon reaches 792 feet. The hilly land continues through Rotherfield to Wadhurst, north of which are the headwaters of the River Teise. Southwards is slightly lower ground at Mayfield and Hadlow Down overlooking the Rother and its tributaries. This country is all typically wooded Wealden ridge and valley landscape—some are almost like ravines—and from the sharp ridges are often very fine views.

We shall begin with Crowborough and work northwards and southwards along the edges of the Forest. Crowborough has been described as a place without charm or interest, and whilst its terrible sprawl is no delight to the eye, it is hardly true to say it has no interest. In fact its rather short history has produced some fascinating—even extraordinary—people and events.

Its spread, apart from past speculation and present poor planning, is mostly due to its lack of a real centre. It grew up Topsy fashion around three small places: Crowborough Town, most of which is within Ashdown Forest; Crowborough Cross on the main A26; and Jarvis Brook eastwards down in a valley around and near the station.

Its origin was a windy hill, presumably with crows as inhabitants, for the name means Crow Hill from O.E. Crawe Bearg, for there was not much else here until the early seventeenth century when Crown land on the Forest edge was sold for small-holdings in the reign of Charles I. These were on land underlain by the sandy Ashdown Beds with silt layers and indifferently drained, being poor by any standards.

There was no village of any kind until Sir Henry Fermor built a chapel in 1732 attached to Rotherfield parish. Fermor was of an old family, originally from Picardy in France, and lived at Walsh Manor, Jarvis Brook, built in 1551, near an old moated enclosure. The name Walsh is from William le Walshe of Rotherfield, and Jarvis Brook comes from Priscilla Jervis of Mayfield. In the 1830s a Robert Burgess Fry lived there and had a manorial holding on Ashdown Forest from the Duchy of Lancaster on payment of two roses. Periodically a representative of the Duchy would call, snip off two roses from a tree at the farmhouse, put them in his buttonhole and walk away; one imagines they must have been red ones. Fermor's chapel became a church with a fine tower, and today a pleasant churchyard with some good oaks and yews, whilst Walsh Manor regrettably seems to have descended to a school for delinquents—with no sign of the moated enclosure in spite of the Department of the Environment calling it a moated site.

There was little more by 1832, when the road from Uckfield to Tunbridge Wells was described as 'very bad, being wholly deep loose sand, but the traveller is compensated by the view from Crowborough Beacon Turnpike'. The Beacon then was bare of trees or houses, but in 1838 an isolated house was built there, with the height (incorrectly) engraved on the wall. It is still there, but now completely engulfed by houses.

In 1839 Earl de la Warr, Lord of the Manor on the Forest, had a church of St John built at what is now Crowborough Town, but belonging to the parish of Withyham.

After this the next few years are best described from the work of Dr C. Leeson-Prince who lived there from 1872, and established a meteorological station, and produced in 1898 *Observations and Climate of Crowborough Hill*. He describes the area fifty years before, when in 1841 many of the poorer inhabitants got a living from cutting litter on the Forest—a very controversial practice, which we shall see later caused lawsuits against the Forest Commoners. Crowborough Cross at that time was described as just a miserable little grocer's shop; it had no

butcher and all meat had to come from Rotherfield. Further
south down the main road to Uckfield opposite the 'Crow and
Gate', there was another pub called the Blue Anchor, which
apparently had inmates so lawless that none dared go near
it—probably the last remnants of the smuggling era.

Leeson-Prince's work as a doctor brought him into contact
with incredible conditions, and once to see an ill woman he had
to crawl into a conical hut on Crowborough Common on his
hands and knees. Another time in the winter, whilst by a bed in
Crowborough attending to a patient, he suddenly felt terribly
cold, and found his feet surrounded by drifted snow through a
broken window, and his horse which had been brought into the
kitchen went and ate all the bread that was in the house. He
remarks sternly that no parson in the Rotherfield parish ever
visited the poor.

Crowborough's speculative era seems to have begun in 1856
when the Goldsmiths' Company bought up some country
gentlemen's estates in the district, which had previously
belonged to members of the company. These were then parcelled
out as building sites, but with strict conditions as to quality and
size of house. The Goldsmith's Company also planted many
pinewoods on the north-east side and edges of Ashdown Forest,
amongst which still are large Victorian houses like those in
Fielden and Warren Roads.

Crowborough in 1860 rather incredibly had an outbreak of
witchcraft, for a man whose wife was pining away consulted a
kind of 'expert' in Tunbridge Wells, a Mr Oakley, for advice. He
was given a cup with a liquid which fizzed, and when it cleared,
the husband cried: 'I see her, 'tis Witch Killick.' There was, it
seems, a Mrs Killick who locally had the reputation of a witch,
who when later dying begged her daughter to come to her and
receive her 'spirit' according to custom. Another strange occur-
rence was a woman churning butter, which would not set so her
son thrust a red-hot poker into the churn which hissed with a
loud scream; later he met a woman, Dame Neve, limping with a
burnt leg!

Crowborough had two windmills; one was Pratts Mill, a tiled
tower mill owned by Richard Pratt, a Baptist minister and
writer, who lost his son Jesse when his frock coat was caught in
the machinery. The mill worked for some forty-five years by

wind, and then until 1922 by steam. The second mill, near Crowborough Beacon, was an old post mill built in 1782, and was burnt down in 1942 during the war.

The railway from Uckfield to Groombridge was opened in 1866, with a station actually at Jarvis Brook, but named Rotherfield as that was the parish name. In 1880 when Crowborough became a parish the station was renamed Crowborough and Jarvis Brook. The line is worth travelling on for there are superb views of Ashdown Forest from the train.

Around the turn of the century many of the small farms which had originated with the Crown land sales in Stuart times fell into the market, and there was another bout of building expensive houses that developed into a rich commuter settlement. By 1904 when the east side of the town was a heap of scaffolding and piles of bricks it was being described as 'Scotland in Sussex'; undeniably it was one of the most healthy places in Sussex.

One of these houses, Warren Gate, was built by a Dr White on the site of an earlier house called Hanover built by the developer of Crowborough Warren, Howis. It is a curious Y-shaped building in Cotswold style, but using local sandstone, and one of the first houses ever to have a damp course. I found its interior to be equally intriguing, because of the Y-shape, and a very roomy place.

In 1909 Sir Arthur Conan Doyle, perhaps Crowborough's most famous inhabitant, built a large new house near the golf course called 'Windlesham Manor'. Everyone knows Sherlock Holmes, but Professor Challenger of *The Lost World* fame, a book deriving from Doyle's geological interests, appears in some less well-known stories set locally. There is one which concerns Rotherfield called 'The Poison Belt'; another on the South Downs called 'When the World Screamed', which uncannily foretold the American attempt to pierce the Earth's mantle by the Mohole Project of the 1960s. The longest was 'Land of the Mist', used as a vehicle for Doyle's spiritualism beliefs, which converts the Professor from scepticism. Much more interesting is the Appendix with actual psychic happenings narrated—far too many to be dismissed lightly.

The most curious of Doyle's writings was published in the *Strand Magazine* of 1922 called 'The Cottingly Fairies'. This concerned two girls in Yorkshire, Elsie Wright and her South African cousin, Frances Griffiths, who over some three years claimed to have 'played with fairies' and took five photographs on plates. These were carefully examined by experts, who found no trace of faking—which in fact would have been very difficult to do—and many people maintained they were genuine; there seems a most curious ring of truth about the whole thing.

Doyle died in 1930, aged seventy-one, and for some years he and his wife were buried in their garden, before finally being placed in the family vault in 1935. I suppose it was inevitable that the place had a reputation of being haunted, and was later exorcized. I went to have a look recently but the atmosphere seemed, if anything, to be very tranquil—although a young girl working in the kitchen (it is now a residential hotel) said she was sensitive to these things, and was not at all sure.

One famous inhabitant of forty years ago was a cockatoo belonging to the Free Church Minister at Crowborough Cross, which flew freely about the streets but always went home to dine and sleep.

Crowborough is now also a Catholic parish, but in its early days in 1910, with neither church nor chapel, Mass was heard in the Oddfellows Hall, and one amusing story relates from this. The screen of the confessional was so unstable that an Irishman used to hold it in place during the hearing of confessions; he was actually stone deaf, but always used to announce the fact in a very loud voice so as not to upset the penitents!

During the First World War Crowborough had a military camp, which is still there, and between the wars there was a murder case worthy of Simenon's Maigret stories. A young poultry farmer was hanged at Lewes in 1925 for cutting up and burying his former fiancée, who he said had hanged herself. There was a fierce legal-cum-medical battle over the case at Lewes, with the famous pathologist Sir Bernard Spilsbury giving evidence; Conan Doyle was one of many who expressed doubts about the man's guilt.

Crowborough's Topsy-like growth seemed also to affect its shops, for in 1935 at Crowborough Cross, next to Lloyds Bank, was one whose name was Pianos and Confectionery, for in one window were grand pianos and in the other was a plate of cakes. A local historian recalled that this was grocery in the medieval sense—which was 'engrossing' one's business—usually trading in oriental spices. Edward III made this kind of trade illegal on account of unfairness to the trade guilds, forerunners of trade unions, and hence our word 'grocer' comes from this—one who was a 'Grosser'.

Even by 1939 the population of this curious amorphous place was only 2,000 and it is since the war that the biggest and perhaps worst urban development has evolved, in spite of planning. Row after row of brick boxes have been badly sited, and the Beacon area has been overwhelmed with the more pretentious kind, so that inevitably the town has lost all contact with Ashdown Forest in spite of its superb site, one of the best in the county.

Northwards from the town out along the road to St John's and Lye Green we come to a bridle path that leads to Gillridge Farm. The name means gold or golden ridge from Gilderigge about 1285, and could refer to the deep yellowish soil of the Tunbridge Wells sands here. It is an interesting case of a place in complete contrast to Crowborough, for it failed to grow. The farm and outlying Oast are the only survivors of an abandoned settlement, which once had a chapel before it was removed to Withyham on Archbishop Peckham's orders in 1292.

The farmstead must have remained isolated for centuries, and but for the motor car would be even now. The farm specializes in fruit—another example of using the light soils of the Ashdown beds around the Forest—but the Oast has forsaken Mother Earth to become an art gallery. All this is in contrast to Orznash a little further along with its farm equipment lying around, and surrounded by woods which have proved very fruitful for finding Roman and medieval ironworking sites. Orznash, once spelt Hoarsnash, means—it seems—Osa's stubble land. The bordering Bream Wood had many notices forbidding riders to stray off the bridleway; this underlines a local problem—the trespassing by horseriding. It is really a symptom of Britain's overcrowded population, people, horses and cars all trying to avoid each other.

From Orznash by footpaths and orchards—pleasant surroundings always—one can reach Boarshead on the main road. Many years ago there was a widow who kept a beerhouse here, and to attract customers she dressed herself in a variety of colours with a fool's cap and feathers and pretended to be tipsy. If the price of beer rises much higher, some customers may be tempted to demand similar entertainment.

At Boarshead a long line of rocky Ardingly sandstone crags outcrop and trend away to Bowles Rocks off down a side road. This was a rock climbing area, which has developed into the Bowles Outdoor Pursuits Centre. It seems very well organized indeed and includes canoeing on the Medway and sailing at Bewl Bridge. I walked around it and peeped at the chapel, a replica of the one on the Matterhorn contributed to twenty years ago by the Swiss and Austrian Alpine Clubs. Seeing all this reminded me of the old Service expression 'everything laid on', and I had a few faint doubts, because for me anything done out of doors ought to have some sense of individual spontaneity.

Southwards from Crowborough along the main A26 Uckfield road are two places of great interest, one historical and the other a modern enterprise. The first is the interesting settlement of Heron's Ghyll and the Roman Catholic parish church of St John the Evangelist, whose history is unusual. In 1866 Coventry Patmore, poet and convert, bought an old large farmhouse of medieval origin called 'Pucksty', a name meaning Pixie's or Fairy's field. It was bought, so it was said, from a man of rather sinister reputation, a Mr Benham, who kept a mistress in a local cottage and had caused his wife to die so that her ghost haunted the house drive, and seven priests had to be called to 'send her to the Red Sea'. This was a local tradition preserved by cottagers on Ashdown Forest.

Patmore also bought the Old Lands estate from Robert Holford, land that had once been part of Ashdown Forest. He then opened a Domestic Oratory, a private Catholic chapel, but had difficulty in getting a resident priest. The name of the house and the subsequent settlement here came about following the many different names that Patmore used during the next three years: Buxted Hall, Old Lands Hall, Old Lands House and at length Heron's Ghyll. This last was due to his having sold Old Lands to a Mr Nesbitt, who started to build a house which he called Oldlands Hall.

Coventry Patmore left Heron's Ghyll in 1874, and after a gap it was bought by the Duke of Norfolk for the Dowager Duchess Mina who built a school and chapel in 1880, and established a pioneer Catholic mission there. She died in 1886, and her grandson James Fitzalan Hope bought the property and in 1897 built the present church (which cost only the extraordinarily low sum of £3,000). This is a beautiful building based on the old pre-Reformation church of St Mary, Clymping, near Little-hampton.

Hope greatly extended the property by acquiring the estates of Stroods, Chillies and Barnsgate until it comprised about 1,000 acres. From 1913 to 1928 there was a small orphanage run by Dominican nuns, and Heron's Ghyll became a parish in 1922. Hope was made Lord Rankeillour in 1932 for his services to the House of Commons, and in 1935 the house was leased to the well-known preparatory school Temple Grove, founded at East Sheen in 1810. My aunt, Mrs MacCarthy (now in Tasmania), lived for about fourteen years in a house called The Camellias in Temple Sheen, East Sheen. The house was built on the site of the original Temple Grove School, and she once saw the ghost of a young man carrying a pile of old books (and wearing plimsolls) whom she supposed to have been a master at the school. The Camellias had a second ghost whose footsteps were often heard by several people—including my wife, much to her astonish-ment.

During this long period Heron's Ghyll parish, originally a mission, covered an enormous area of Sussex from Sheffield Park and most of Ashdown Forest across almost to Mayfield. Later the parishes of Uckfield and Crowborough were taken from it, and today Heron's Ghyll covers the southern half of Ashdown.

I talked to the present priest-in-charge, Canon Joseph Tritscher, who later showed me this splendid little church, which has some particularly beautiful windows. Inside it is difficult to realize that the church is so young, for there is a curious feeling of ancient sanctity here, and a writer on East Sussex has remarked, unconscious of its origin, 'It looks more C. of E. than Roman.'

The second place to see is Barnsgate Vineyard, the inheritor of a property which was once part of Heron's Ghyll and now has 21½ acres of very varied types of grapes. This is quite different from the normal English vineyard, of which I have seen quite a few and also written about. It is a thoroughly sound commercial wine producer owned by the Peyroth family with 300 years of experience behind them as the largest private German vineyard owners. The wine is sold through private wine tastings and they have opted for quality, so their wines will hardly be cheap. I have had two visits here, the first on a bright day in October when they were harvesting—the *vendange* in French. English has no exact equivalent, so we must invent a word; what about 'grapeage'? This was particularly interesting for they were red wine grapes, Pinot Noir, and I asked the efficient, well-trained and obviously enthusiastic, Mr Richard Evans, what sort of wine he would make. 'I am not sure,' he said, 'might be a red, or *rosé*, but it will certainly be fresh, young and clean.'

Later I had a more professional visit and saw wine being made; 1982's crop is the best since 1976, and they are hoping here to make some really good wine. Mr Evans explained that with the run of poor summers we have been having, if the 'wood' of the vine has not ripened the year before to produce buds and flowers, even if a good summer follows the vines will not produce much.

I was intrigued by the varieties of grapes being grown—six acres of Chardonnais—the Chablis grape—sounded strange for an English vineyard, but Chablis itself is quite far north. The site of Barnsgate is high, just above the 500 feet contour, but this means it is frost-free, and as it faces south catches what sunshine is going. The soils, however, are not good—not that that means much where vines are concerned—but here they need draining, and they are exposed because of the height. In a good year the wine will be good, which is not tautology for the combination of height and sun will make the difference compared with some other vineyards.

The medieval farmhouse here is an attractive building, and an old German wine press of 1834 with Jesus-Mary-Joseph inscribed on it reminds us that vignerons are or used to be God-fearing people, which is not a bad idea when your livelihood depends so much upon the elements.

Further down the A26, which is one of the very few main roads now in Sussex that is worth travelling along for there is so much of interest, we shall come to Hendall Wood on our right, a beautiful stretch of trees that was cut down some years ago by a Brighton brewer notorious for his speculations. Further felling has reduced it even more, but there is still some left.

Opposite here down a lane is Bevingford, a fifteenth-century hall house. The south wing has gone, but the north one was extended in 1606. In front is a delightful little walled sunken garden. The land around was farmed for fifty years by Mr and Mrs Grant, a long time in Sussex these days, and seemed about the right size for a farm—133 acres; they had left only the day before and I talked to a farmworker made redundant. He was not worried, his is a job still in demand in these days of unemployment. The name Bevingford does not refer to a stream but means enclosure of Beofa's people (O.E. Beabinga-worp), and nowadays is a pleasant backwater.

Back up the main road once more, we turn eastwards along a lane which leads to Tudor Rocks, and yet another outcrop of Ardingly sandstone, where suddenly it is quite wild with holly, brambles, birch and gorse on the poor acid sandy soil. I thought that this sort of terrain would be excellent for cantering with a horse, and as if someone had read my thoughts two riders appeared with cheerful Sussex accents and galloped past the rocks and round a soggy field. These sandstone outcrops have caused a local mystery, for round the corner in the Buxted to High Hurstwood Road is a house called The Hermitage. In the grounds is or was (for it is some time since I saw it) a cave dwelling of two hollowed-out rooms with ledges and niches which was thought to have been the cell of an anchorite or hermit.

This is but one of some interesting and very varied houses along this three-mile-long wooded road from Buxted to the A26 Crowborough Road. Beginning at the Buxted end is what is now called Olive House, divided into two. It is a curious three-storey building, part Tudor but with a much later hung-tiled upper part with a hipped roof. No less mixed were some of the owners, for when I first knew the house it was an orphanage called Fegan House. My sister was the matron there, and as domestic help was in short supply she used to get the boys to polish the floors by 'skating', that is by attaching cloths to their feet and away they went; they loved it, and certainly did not regard such polishing as 'work'.

Later the house was bought by the British Anarchist Society, who already had the farm next door and who had been strange neighbours when it was Fegan House. Now it is owned by a retired Colonial Office administrator who assures me that it has returned to its original name of Olive House.

Past Hermitage and here is High Hurstwood—not an old place, but probably an old name, which could mean high enclosed wood (O.E. *heeg*—hurst), but with so many variants on old documents and deeds—Hayhurst (1602), Haighurst—it may not mean high at all. The oldest building was thought to be a forester's cottage, probably when the whole area flanked Ashdown, not far from the church (built in 1870, about when it became a parish). Coventry Patmore risked excommunication, so he joked, when he presented the church with one of its bells, placed in a bell turret on the roof, and not in the later tower of 1903.

Further along is an old quarry with a fine outcrop of Ashdown sandstone, and you can see the junction with the overlying Wadhurst Clay. A house has been built within the old workings and rather well landscaped; I saw it in March with many crocuses and it all looked very fine.

On the left higher up the road is a cottage on a little bank, a sandstone building with a slate roof and brick chimney, the date of the building 1853. Nothing unusual in that you may say, but it was a significant change, for the ordinary house was gradually beginning then to use the cheaper, durable Welsh slates and mass-produced bricks, rather than local Sussex materials.

Eastwards from Crowborough a typical up and down Wealden road, the B2100, takes us to Rotherfield, once within the bounds of Ashdown Forest. The village stands high on a ridge at over 500 feet and is a very old place, and once was a very large parish; the name is derived from Hrythera feld, meaning a clearing for cattle—a rare name in the Weald and there are only four examples.

By Domesday it had become Redrefelle, and was a heavily forested royal estate from King Alfred's time until William I, and later passed to the powerful Nevills; Waterdowne, Eridge and Rotherfield were continuous and all part of the manor of Rotherfield. The church site is old, eighth century, and along with a priory was dedicated to St Denis in France, but these foundations are lost in the mists of time. The present church of St Denys is large and impressive, with a fifteenth-century tower, heavily battlemented. Inside are the vestiges of medieval murals with various scenes from the Scriptures, this being then the manner of teaching them.

Rotherfield is a watershed for nearby is the source of the Rother, traditionally flowing out of the cellar of a house; and the headwaters of the Ouse (Uckfield River) and the Teise flow down its slopes. South and east are large outcrops of iron-bearing Wadhurst Clay, for here and around our next village, Wadhurst, was the scene of ironworking for nearly 2,000 years: Celtic, Roman, medieval and finally Tudor. Today it still seems a real village, with many pleasantly varied styles of houses all crouching next to each other (as proper villages should have), and it has a Georgian pub, the Royal Arms, to refresh you whilst you contemplate its ancestry. The village is famous for a lady who broke an all-male tradition, for here lived the first woman doctor Sophia Jex Blake (1840–1912).

From the village a number of ridge routes radiate; northwards through wooded country one goes to the old Redgate Mill in a deep valley—at one time seen much better by train. Northeastwards you dip down again to Town Row, a little satellite hamlet where once, sadly, was the railway station on the beautifully scenic Cuckoo Line, which might have celebrated its centenary, but for the death sentence pronounced in the Beeching Report of 1963. Even in 1965 there were 250 passengers a day on the line in spite of extraordinary efforts to discourage traffic. Some railway historians writing about 'forgotten railways' seem themselves to have forgotten that the old companies never intended that these branch lines should pay. Their main lines balanced their deficits; they were in effect indirect social services—as indeed many things are today, as though it was something quite new.

Nearby Bletchinglye Farm presents with its name an interesting derivation, for it could be connected with the Surrey place-name, or with cattle being brought here from the manor of East Blatchington (near Seaford) which was a forest pasture for the people of Blaeca.

From Town Row it is a climb again up to Mark Cross on a ridge at 518 feet. The name here is simple enough being the boundary or mearc between the three parishes of Rotherfield, Mayfield and Wadhurst. There is an excellent pub here, the

Mark Cross Inn, very fashionable and therefore sometimes crowded, but a good place to pause before exploring further. Northwards along the A267 in Nap Wood, a National Trust Nature Reserve open on Sundays from April to October. It is a genuine fragment of Wealden wildwood with its mature oaks, birch and pine with alder woods along the stream at the bottom. I saw it in early July and so there were not many birds in evidence, but I did find the marsh violet—although prolonged searching failed to produce the golden saxifrage which is amongst the wetland flora. The paths wind through the ravines of the sandstone, but unfortunately there is far too much bracken in the wood which needs clearing, but the voluntary labour to do this job is simply not forthcoming, even in these days of unemployment, and in spite of the existence of Conservation Volunteers.

From here I walked across the fields to have a look at the Tudor mansion of 'Lightlands' with its connections with Ashdown Forest and ironworking, and that of Riverhall reached further on by footpaths. On the way there by road—a roundabout route—there is a most lovely Wealden house called 'Partridges', dated 1485, with a large lawn and a few cherry trees.

Coming back from this long foray I got lost trying to return via Nap Wood, but at length reached the main road where, incredibly for a Sunday in July, I saw at very close quarters a wild fallow deer standing on the deserted road. After mutual stares it disappeared into the wooded slopes of Saxonbury Hill.

This is a stiff but worthwhile climb up to its summit at 663 feet, where amid masses of rhododendrons like mangrove swamps, and rising above the trees, is a circular tower. This was built in 1828, with a staircase, now removed, and the interesting roof is forlornly broken down and dilapidated. The view at the top over Ashdown and the High Weald must have been a rare sight, and it is a great pity we cannot go up and see over the most forested region of these islands. Here on Saxonbury is the highest point of the High Weald east of Ashdown, and not for nothing did the ancient Iron Age Celts build their fortified camp here.

Back to Mark Cross and southwards from Rotherfield via Castle Hill steep descents bring us to a valley of a tributary of the Uckfield Ouse, and at Stone Mill a footpath leads along the valley to two farms. The first, Hugget's Furnace Mill Farm, has a Victorian farmhouse, but there is a very old mill building in the yard by the valley track. This is the remains of the water mill, an inheritor of earlier ironworking, which in turn became the first steam-operated mill. I talked to the farmer, who had been one of the agricultural negotiators for Britain's entry into the European Community, and a firm believer in our membership, for many varied reasons, and learnt that he at one time farmed intensively here, but was now 'slowing down' and farming at a gentler pace.

Next door is Hugget's Furnace Farm, where the farmhouse in complete contrast regarding age for it is a real gem of a medieval building—certainly the best I have ever been lucky enough to visit. The farmer's wife told me that they had lived there about ten years, but used to be at Birchden Forge, Eridge, which they had restored. Walking round the inside of this marvellous house it was not hard to imagine a very long bygone Sussex. It had been lived in by an ironmaster, but was obviously much older than the Tudor furnace here. The farmer here farmed on the 'dog and stick' principle—that is, certainly not intensively—and had a herd of old English Longhorns bred at Bakewell, Derbyshire, from the oldest Park White breed. He had not weeded one of his fields and during the earlier drought in the year the weeds and thistles had provided some feed for cattle, when other farmers' fields were almost bare.

I shall be referring to both these farms again in the chapter on ironworking. For me they both vindicated my contention that far too much of Britain is farmed too intensively with masses of mechanical equipment paid for or borrowed at high interest rates, and with too many large farms for such a small country. In reality it is high-cost farming, and its much publicized efficiency ought to be measured by profit per acre coupled with the farmer's own expectations and a readiness to live within his means. And the much criticized German part-time farmers are just as efficient, if not more so, even if their costs are high—which is an accident of currency not expense—and who farm as a way of life not as agro-businessmen.

South-east of Rotherfield is the windy height of Argos Hill, on which stands a well-restored white post mill with a Sussex tailpole fan tackle. It dates from 1825, having been worked continuously for eighty-eight years by a local family, the Westons. The site is old and in 1656 was known as Argatt's Hill from the O.E. personal name Eardgar, which rather shows how a name can come to mean something quite different.

Back to Mark Cross again, and eastwards along the Wadhurst road is Frankham, first the woods on the left full of minepits dug in the Wadhurst Clay for iron and marl, and then oaks and coppiced chestnuts rising to enormous heights making for a real forest. Frankham Park next door once belonged to the Archbishop's Palace at Mayfield, and had over 9 acres of fish ponds for the fasting prelates; but that was long ago, and now in the grounds is a Greek open-air theatre set among an old apple orchard and an ash grove.

Over the road whilst walking to Sandyden Ghyll by the footpath I suddenly caught the delicious scent of hay, and sure enough there were two people haymaking, but not it seems for cattle—for horses instead—and they were having great trouble with the mechanical baler. I recalled memories of haymaking in high summer in North Devon many years before with a horse and cart, and the farmer's wife and daughter bringing out a huge cream tea to eat in the field and later, suitably refreshed, we worked on to 11 p.m., to get all the hay in.

From Frankham past Beggar's Bush and the 1888 Wadhurst College in South Hill to Wadhurst itself; still a pleasant enough place, but overflowing with commuters, as the outside of the station with its vast concourse of parked cars testifies. The station itself is a fine little building of 1852 with pediments, whose architect, W. Trees, was quite famous in his day. The line here was due to be electrified in 1985, but there are vague rumours of closure—one shudders at the chaos that would cause.

Wadhurst, whose name rather simply means Wada's hyrst or wooded hill, was as most people know one of the great centres of the Tudor iron industry, and it is in the church of St Peter and St Paul where the best evidence is displayed. This is a fine building with its 128-foot broached spire of shingled cedar wood rising out of the Norman tower with a very fine, but silent, clock. Broached spires rise from the tower without parapets, and they are quite common in the Weald.

Inside are thirty iron graveslabs of great variety in workmanship ranging from 1617 to 1799, almost the end of the industry in Sussex; and no other church has so many. One reminded me of my researches in Kent on the Colepepper family, for it was to the daughter 'Frances Porter d. 1717 of Sir William Colepepyr Bar. of Aylsford, Kent', mute testimony to a widespread and powerful Wealden family.

I found the village too crowded so went off to look for the nineteenth-century iron mines in Snape Wood in the ridge and vale country of deep Sussex. They were difficult to find for most of the horizontal galleries have now been covered over, but the walk through bluebells, herb robert and wild garlic was pleasant enough. These old mine workings were apparently great favourites of the local lads who used to play cards there, for they were cool in the summer, and warm in the winter.

Whilst searching for the tiny one-time Miner's Arms pub I came upon Snape Cottage where I met someone who might have qualified for the old TV game of 'What's My Line?' This was a Ministry of Agriculture Bee Diseases Inspector, an ex-RAF pilot, who had been made redundant in his civilian job and whose hobby had become his job. Here I learnt that the honey bee is only one of twenty varieties, and that they are complicated creatures to deal with: when glutted with honey they have to be smoked out, and they are quite savage in a thunderstorm.

I found the pub, now a private house, and came across a large splendid Wealden building called Stream Cottage at Scrag Oak. The owner, George Wilde, would perhaps be considered eccentric; his forbears were Irish and he was born and brought up in Kent, apprenticed to a whitesmith, that is a skilled worker in copper, brass and zinc. He is essentially a man of principle and prepared to suffer for it, which he had, and above all he is a great traveller—by train and bicycle—all over Europe.

He and his hospitable wife Marjorie live in a house that was once two cottages dating from 1440, and lay empty, incredibly, for fifteen years—when nobody was in the least interested in Wealden buildings. The roof was once thatched, but now has tiles laid on rafters that came from Holland Park House in 1946, and look as if the roof had never been any other way. Of course, many of the best buildings are often composites and made of cannibalized material; it is the manner of doing that really matters. The mixture called wattle and daub has often fascinated me; now I know how the daub is made, according to George Wilde: sandy loam locally from Snape Wood, mutton trimmings, linseed oil, salt, washing soda and lime!

Inside there is an oak staircase that strikes the eye; this time the oak was local from Lord Courthope's estate at Whiligh, the same place that provided the oak for restoring Westminster Hall over the centuries. George got his in payment for repairing his lordship's vintage car some years back, and an old wheelwright Mr Basset, the uncle of the blacksmith we shall meet in Wadhurst in Chapter 9, made the actual stairs. Of two other objects that were unusual, one which I thought was a bellows turned out to be a foghorn loud-hailer of the type my grandfather, a master mariner in sail until the 1920s, could have used, and the other was either a Sussex chit or a Kentish dole axe, whichever you prefer. You do not know? Neither did I; it is in fact a cleaver for cutting chestnut wood, and was bought for 2/11 in Wadhurst before the war.

The garden was equally intriguing with fruit trees like the blue mussel plum from Smallhythe, and the rare green apple tree with large fruit called a Norfolk Greening. In the meadow were some donkeys that George takes care of, and sitting over coffee in the garden he regaled me with some highly amusing stories about local high life, most of which I regret I cannot reveal.

Just a step from here, but a steep one up the road, is the fine Jacobean farmstead of Wenbans, with a sixteenth-century barn that has traditional diagonal bracing. The name is from the O.E. Wonesbarn meaning Waenan's stream, which fits for not far away are the headstreams of the Rother. Over half a century ago this house was a favourite place to stay for the then Prince of Wales (Duke of Windsor), and from here if you follow the footpath through very pleasant countryside you arrive at Wadhurst Park estate, which has a very high deer fence round most of the area. This is now a modern deer park, following in the tradition of the medieval times in the Weald: the Royal Forest of Ashdown had the largest deer park. The house, once called Wadhurst Hall, is large and does not appear very old; it was visited by the Spanish Ambassador and also used by royalty, this time Edward VII. Before the last war, each time the lodge gates were opened an old lady in a red cloak—an estate pensioner—used to appear.

The way from Wadhurst Park to Tidebrook is along a ridge and then sharply down through Riseden by a steep little valley of a Rother headwater, a most picturesque and rural spot. The name means Tida's meadows, appropriately enough for there are water meadows along the valley bottom. There are also one or two good houses near here; one I saw over was Newhouse Farm, a traditional building but heavily altered during the 1930s. The owner's wife, Mrs Baldwin, pointed out that this conversion would be difficult to 'undo', because being before the present trend to more authentic restoration the workmanship and materials used were of high quality, although rather philistine in character.

Beyond Tidebrook the road is a switchback route to Mayfield on its ridge, at 469 feet, but any effort you make to reach here is well rewarded for with its buildings and views it is the most charming and delightful place that will appear in this book.

Beginning with the name, which is compound one of O.E. *maegthe*, mayweed (chamomile) of the daisy family, plus feld, we have open land where the mayweed grows—it was probably a very early cleared ridge within the forest. Therefore the site is old, a church being founded here in AD 960; this was a *lignea Ecclesia*, a log church built by St Dunstan, Archbishop of Canterbury, a saint whose activities as an ironworking monk have given rise to many legends.

However, the most important building is the Archbishop's Palace—Mayfield being attached to the See of Canterbury since the early ninth century. The last archbishop to live here was Wareham (1502–32). Cranmer surrendered it to the Crown in 1545, and it was granted by Henry VIII to Sir Edward North who sold it in 1546 to Sir Thomas Gresham, the financial magnate and ironmaster. It surpassed all his other houses in magnificence, containing furniture valued at £7,553, a huge sum then. In 1573 he entertained Queen Elizabeth and built a special staircase for her alone. Later he sold the building to the Mayfield ironmaster, Baker, whom we have met earlier. The Bakers lived here from 1617 to 1796, and although still in the family, it became a ruin and was sold yet again in 1858, and then later bought by the Duchess of Leeds, an American heiress, who gave it to the Society of the Holy Child founded by Cornelia Connelly, a Catholic pioneer of girls' education.

This was on condition that the building was restored, which was well carried out by Edwin Pugin who converted the magnificent fourteenth-century hall into a chapel. Later Peter Paul Pugin added a refectory, cloisters and red-brick convent school (1898), but from all that I heard here these later additions are not regarded with great affection.

I had the privilege of being shown the hall by 93-year-old Sister Mary Paul (Nora O'Connor), a Cambridge graduate and a most alert and intelligent old lady. A very fine painted crucifix from Siena in Italy (about 1350), and a 1460 Flemish Madonna adorn the hall, where lies the tomb of Cornelia Connelly. Amongst the exhibits shown to me were a Sussex wafer, an extraordinary heavy piece of ironwork; Princess Victoria's riding whip from when she visited Mayfield in 1836 before becoming Queen; and of course the traditional iron tongs by which St Dunstan held the Devil's nose.

The school has become all that its founder would have wished with a high academic record, well balanced by music, sport (especially riding) and social responsibility.

Outside, the main street has hardly a building in it less than good, and most are quite outstanding. Next to the fifteenth-century convent gatehouse is the Stone House, used by the nuns as a guest-house and called by them Sir Joseph. Its name has a double meaning for it was built by a family called Stone in the 1730s from dressed stone taken from the old Palace ruins.

Over the road at the top is Yeomans, a fifteenth-century hall house with a fine front garden; then comes Walnut Tree House of the same age; and, as its name denotes, right in the centre is Middle House Hotel of 1575, with beautiful carved and moulded brackets on its gables. And worth a good hard stare are Stone Court of 1641 and the London House of mixed age: older seventeeth-century gables and white painted tiles with newer eighteenth-century weather-boarding.

The church, which stands back and is a fine building, replaced its predecessor destroyed by fire in 1389. Inside are some iron graveslabs, one rather intriguingly to an early eighteenth-century owner of wine cellars at St Paul's, who could not read or write, and some appropriate memorials to the Baker family.

One a personal note (as an ex-submariner) I was interested in the badge of H.M. Submarine Tetrarch lost in 1941 in the Mediterranean.

The whole village is compact, and down a short lane you will find a car park, but no ordinary one for this has a superb view across the wooded ridges and distant Rother valley. Further along the side road is a pub called The Brewer's Arms which claims an even finer view, and beyond are some very pleasant cottages. Outside one of them with white weather-boarding, and fuchsias round the door, I met the postman's wife, Mrs Wicker. Her husband keeps bees, so once again the talk was about them! This time it was honey, which in 1982 had not been good; all the blossom was too early, it seems, and honey gathered late does not keep.

Here was a lady who missed the railway and who thought how much nicer the train ride to Eastbourne was for the children, the bus service being poor and finishing far too early. I wondered if those so eager to close branch lines ever really meet people like Mrs Wicker, who had lived in Mayfield for twenty-seven years. She added rather sadly that it was now a rich village with the inevitable commuters' cars and some heavy main road traffic on the A267 which detracted from the village's idyllic appearance.

I thought too of the now long-forgotten 'Captain Swing' labourers' revolt in the autumn of 1830, when the villages round Ashdown Forest like Mayfield, Rotherfield and Buxted were desperate in their poverty and lived on turnips—sometimes just the rinds—and hot water stained with tea.

So to cheer myself up I went down to the old station, a late Victorian building with some rather fine coloured windows and fanlights, and to see some new houses being built which pleasantly surprised me with their hipped roofs, tiles and weather-boarding.

The side road here from Mayfield runs on to Woolbridge, crossing the young Rother stream, and at Horleigh Green a diversion can be made to see some magnificent crags of Ashdown sandstone in Under Rockes Wood that are 30 feet high and run westwards for nearly a mile to the river valley seen earlier at Hugget's Furnace.

4

The Southern Villages

The southern flanks of Ashdown Forest are rather different in character from the other fringes, for although it is still hilly until south of Uckfield the land is lower and eventually merges into the Weald Clay lowland, then the distant South Downs and finally the coastal plain.

Perhaps from the Forest crests the crowded coastal zone seems far off, but somehow the influence of its large resorts and urbanized villages is felt once you have reached Uckfield.

South-westwards the land slopes away from the Forest into the wide valley of the Ouse and its tributaries; but in contrast away to the east it rises through Buxted to the ridge at Cross-in-Hand 531 feet up, and this sandy ridge of Ashdown Beds continues to the sea at Hastings.

Leaving the Forest at Horney Common (the name means corner of enclosed land), the best way to approach the village of Maresfield today is by crossing the B2026 road from Duddleswell, and taking a side road right into the middle of the village, thus avoiding the noisy A22 Eastbourne road. Modern Maresfield is the victim of road renumbering, perhaps unforeseen, as some years ago the A272 was diverted through its main street by renumbering the old B2102 to avoid congestion at Uckfield. Now both places are hideously crowded and noisy with the ever-passing traffic.

The name Maresfield comes from the O.E. mere's field,

meaning open land of or by the pool, which suggests that in times long past its two Ouse tributaries may have been ponded up somewhere; and they certainly were in Tudor times because of the ironworks. The place was a royal manor and an old parish long connected with Ashdown Forest, whose landowners within the parish, large or small, had rights of common. Apparently St Bartholomew's Church was repaired with Forest oaks in Henry VIII's time, quite illegally; and today little is left of its Norman foundation, just a small window in the nave. I found it dark inside, its most interesting items being an iron graveslab of Robert Brooks (1667), and some unusual references to South American missions.

Maresfield, however, has an interesting history and one way of seeing some of it is to take two walks, the first by going into Maresfield Park. There is no park now—it was built on quite some time back—but there are still woods, open land and a pond as well as some good houses of no great age. The main house, called the Park House, belonged to Sir John Villiers Shelley, who may have been related to the poet; he added rooms to an earlier house called The Cross. This was the home of William Newnham, who enclosed Pippingford Park in the seventeenth century, and the property passed to the Shelleys by his daughter's marriage. The Shelleys were Forest Commoners and in the nineteenth century were very active in supporting Commoner's rights, for all that in 1875 they owned 4,000 acres of Sussex land.

The property passed to the son-in-law of the last Lady Shelley, a Mr Pechell, and he in turn, having no heirs, left it to his great friend Count Munster, a German nobleman. Count Munster was a model landlord, greatly liked and respected by his tenants, and so it must have been a minor tragedy when his property was sequestered in 1914 because of the war and his nationality.

Later it was acquired by a Brighton brewer, whom we heard about at Hendall Wood in Chapter 3 and who was notorious for his speculations, his activities being described in 1940 by a local historian as 'without regard to the true interests of the country-side', which reflects the damage done to Sussex in between the wars. At that time the estate had been partly developed as a residential area of good-class houses, which has since continued, making it now a rather exclusive area.

It is interesting to recall that in the early years of the nineteenth century there was a great deal of 'squatting' in Maresfield Park; by 1810 there were 130 separate new enclosures, some of 'hovels and hedges' which the local land-owners dubbed 'an Indian town'. These huts, built often of turf (sod huts), were centres of unrest during the labourers' revolt of 1830—the famous Captain Swing riots—and although the huts were repeatedly pulled down, they were still being rebuilt in the 1870s.

From Maresfield Park over the fields towards Forge Wood is the stream known here as Batts Brook, where at one time was a Tudor iron forge called Lower Marshalls.

We can return to Maresfield by the pond in the park and begin the second walk from behind the churchyard and through Park Farm. Here is an early oast kiln (1755), quite unlike the more familiar variety, this being built of dressed ashlar stone.

Further along, the route passes through a wood not far from a stream where there is a little wild area of marshy alders and birch trees, and soon you come to a beautiful lake with reeds and water lilies. This was the old Maresfield Furnace Pond, now private fishing, but a peep at it will not harm the fish. The furnace itself was at the other end, near where Batts Brook comes in.

The furnace was famous for gun casting and in 1608 James I tried to smelt twenty tons of silver ore brought from Scotland, which failed so it went back to Scotland again, but this time taking with it a skilled Sussex foundryman. Eventually the works here became a powder mill, which lasted until 1854, until it went the way of many—a violent explosion—and that was that.

Back in the village, pause amid the traffic and see the tile-hung cottages and the fine Georgian pub, The Chequers, before continuing down the side road and taking the A272 to Buxted at Coopers Green.

Buxted Park comes first, and you will be glad to escape into it if you have come along this road in the rush hour. At the entrance is the celebrated Hogge House of 1581 with the hog rebus on the north wall. The house is large with three bays, but I suspect much rebuilt, and surrounded by a fine walled garden. It

"Image of the Wealden Forest", Tunbridge Wells

The Elephant Rock, The Warren, Eridge Rocks. (Waterdowne Forest)

Cochford Farm, Hartfield (the house of A. A. Milne)

Poohsticks Bridge, Steel Forge River, Hartfield

Argos Hill Windmill,
Rotherfield

Stream Cottage, Scrag
Oak, Wadhurst

The Piltdown
Man

Fletching
Church

Colin Godmans,
Furners Green

Wapsbourne Farm, Sheffield Park

The Ouse Viaduct, near Balcombe

Ashdown Sandstone,
Ecclesbourne Glen,
Hastings

Soil erosion, Ashdown Forest

Pine clump in the snow, Ashdown Forest

The Mediaeval Pale, near
Legsheath Farm,
Ashdown Forest

John of Gaunt, original
owner of Lancaster Great
Park

belonged to Ralph Hogge, of course, the famous ironmaster, who cast the first Sussex cannon, but not in Buxted—the old fable that so many books keep repeating; this is discussed in Chapter 9 on ironworking.

On the other side is a curious little gatehouse at the park entrance with a porticoed doorway and fanlights, red-brick and wooden Corinthian columns, an extremely neat and attractive dwelling. Buxted Park is large and was once an old manor with a long history of owners. The main house, once Buxted Place but now called Buxted Park, has had a chequered history since it was built about 1750 by Edward Medley and completed by his nephew George, a rich wine merchant who lost part of his fortune in the Lisbon earthquake of 1755. It became the property of the Earl of Liverpool, through marriage, and in the early nineteenth century he wanted the people of the old village, then inside the park, to move and join the new village being built along the main road. They refused to go, so he drove them out by refusing to repair their houses; it was 1836 before the last houses were cleared away and the park enclosed. The house was improved and had Georgian additions from London and Norfolk, brought by Basil Ionides, a later owner, but was almost destroyed by fire in 1940, and soldiers billeted nearby guarded the entrances with fixed bayonets to keep out sightseers.

The wife of Basil Ionides was the daughter of Marcus Samuel, 1st Lord Bearsted. His father had a Whitechapel factory which made wooden shell-covered boxes for souvenirs in seaside resorts. Marcus Samuel inherited the business in 1870, but not caring for it formed the 'Shell' Petrol Company, calling his product after the family business, and thus began the vast Royal Anglo-Dutch Shell concern.

Buxted House was repaired, became institutional with its appearance now rather ordinary, except for the entrance countryard, and was at length bought by Sheik Zayed-bin-Sultam-Al-Nayham, from one of the United Emirates of the Gulf, traditional allies of Britain. He completely refurbished it, though he rarely visits it—the last time was in 1975.

However, I have been lucky enough to have a peep inside, and there is only one word that describes it: magnificent. Although a cinema, radio room, and sauna have been added, I do not think the eighteenth-century owners would be at all displeased. The view from the back of a long grassy avenue between trees is all that one imagines from an English stately home.

The nearby large parish church of St Margaret the Queen (of Scotland, 1045–93) is approached by an avenue of lime trees, and is a fine church both inside and in appearance. It has been in the Archbishop of Canterbury's patronage for over 1,300 years and was the centre of a large parish now divided into seven. Outside, the short but fine thirteenth-century spire seems to fit the large building, and inside the original barrel roof is plastered over with an elegant design of marguerite daisies and hop flowers done in 1600, given by the Rector in gratitude for a crop of hops that was unusually good. Hops were grown at this time much more in Sussex than in Kent; and their decline afterwards may well have been caused by the deterioration in the climate (especially on these exposed ridges of the High Weald) which continued until about 1750.

The other unusual item is a very large beadle's church mace of about 1800, with which one supposes he asserted his dignity.

Outside in the churchyard is an enormous yew estimated at over a thousand years old, and to the west within the park are the remains of the medieval village street—a hollow way. North-east of the church is a terrace dated by thirteenth-century pottery and discovered by Mr C. F. Tebbutt, the Ashdown Forest archaeologist.

Modern Buxted is more or less at the top of the next hill after crossing the valley of the Uckfield Ouse, where near the station there is a good pub, the Georgian White Hart. The village today, though dull, seems prosperous enough, and no echo remains of the troubles 150 years ago when Buxted was one of the villages around the Forest where feeling ran so high.

One of the deeper reasons was manifested on 28th August 1830 when there was rioting and wholesale destruction of threshing machines throughout the area; it was because the machines dispensed with winter labour and forced the workless on to the parish. It seems ironical that England, which had pioneered the great agricultural improvements, now had these problems, but of course the increase in enclosure had enabled them to come about. At the same time they caused the landless labourer at the end of an agricultural hierarchy of large landowner, large tenant, small tenant.

Conditions got worse as a result of the Napoleonic Wars and Buxted, like some other villages, became a centre of smuggling, for the humblest participant in 'free trade' was better off than the half-starved farmworkers. Many of those involved—high to low—did not regard themselves at war with French people merely because the governments were, and 500 English smugglers were working out of Dunkirk bringing in smuggled gold to pay for the goods denied by high tariffs and war. The peace of 1815 did not help for suddenly 150,000 demobbed seamen were let loose and smuggling actually increased, but by 1830 was in rapid decline—ironically another reason for rural poverty.

From Buxted the ridge climbs up to Hadlow Down, an old name from a forest clearing again (Headda's clearing), another place with old houses; but a newer parish, for the church dates from 1856 and was rebuilt in 1913 in an attractive Wealden style. One house here is rather remarkable having formed part of the Nevill estate at Eridge and therefore emblazoned with the Nevill heraldry, and known as Old Hadlow House. It was originally a Tudor Hall house and much later extended in the early nineteenth century to a building with no less than sixty rooms and with Georgian fronts being put on the wings.

South of the ridge is a maze of side roads, one of which leads past Shepherd's Hill, near where there is a curious water-filled moat with a long stone parapet whose origin is mysterious.

Then via Pounsley, which is a subject for the ironworking chapter, and down to Blackboys, where the inn on the Lewes road was once a fourteenth-century farmhouse. Here in Blackboys down a lane off the Waldron road is a dairy farm with an unusual feature called the Dower House Farm Trail. Mr Desmond Gunner has organized round his 500-acre farm a 3-mile walk which allows you to see the normal farming activities together with other inhabitants of the land such as wild animals, birds, plants and trees, all to be disturbed as little as possible. This walk takes in a lake which is a wildfowl sanctuary, an old hornbeam coppice used as a shelter belt, a badger's sett, a Scots pine plantation used as a nursery for beech, a pasture field unseeded since 1954, and a woodland with many different planted trees like alder, lime, field maple, guelder rose—just to name a few—and all this will cost you nothing. It is an idea that some other large farms could well copy, for it allows the encouragement of a more natural environment, but at the same time produces food.

Blackboys' name is a puzzle as there are four possibilities: first from the Norman French *blanc bois* (silver birch) and then becoming corrupted; second from 'black boys' from ironworking and charcoal burning; third—real ones, that is negroes; and lastly from Richard Blakeboy, a fifteenth-century squire who lived there.

A summertime diversion from here is to Cross-in-Hand, where there is a mill which stopped working in 1969 when a stock broke. Since then it is gradually, but with difficulty, being restored. I talked with the mill owner, Mr Newnham—a Sussex name which has had many connections with Ashdown Forest's history—about his problems of repairing the stock (the wooden shaft to which the sweeps are attached). The best wood is American long leaf pine, impossible to get now, so they may have to use steel, which somehow does not seem right.

Mr Newnham has written a splendid little book on the mill's history, from which I learnt that the site dates from 1264, and about the families who worked it, as well as a history of milling and the corn trade. One local point of interest was that at the turn of the century the mill used to produce grain for chickens and the 'Cuckoo Line' ran a special chicken train every night, and in 1893 Uckfield Station alone shifted over 1,000 tons of chickens.

Whilst talking with him about wind and water power, he said how Britain had neglected her rivers and streams, which we could harness for many small local sites to generate electricity, instead of the mammoth power stations which have so disfigured the landscape.

Back to Blackboys and towards Framfield on the left is a side road leading to Newplace Farm. On the way is a wood which in late spring was all bluebells, oaks, wild rhododendrons and chestnuts with cuckoos calling. And in here is another listed medieval moated site, probably a fish stew, the outline of which my wife recognized quite clearly. More and more of these moats are coming to light, like those of Blackham Court and Frankham Park mentioned earlier, which is revealing about the medieval diet; probably the fish were mostly carp, as other freshwater fish in England tend to be at best dull and bony—I have heard them described as tasting like muddy blotting paper and hairpins!

Southwards is a very pretty ornamental lake at Newplace Farm, once connected with ironworking. And so via the B2101 to Framfield, a small and very pleasant village, but which in its centre has some new low-density buildings that do not match at all. Once again economic priority spoils visual harmony—or perhaps people do not mind or care?

There is one remarkable medieval house (about 1400) here called Beckets, with a Victorian tower roofed with hand-made hung tiles; the effect is harmonious and quite exciting. The eighteenth-century Framfield Place is now flats amid a reedy lake with an air of faint decay, offset by some fine trees including a Chile pine.

The church of St Thomas-à-Becket has a Horsham slate roof and was minus its tower for 225 years when the old one collapsed in 1667. The oldest part of the church, dating from 1288, is the Hempstead Chapel named from an old farm to the north. One feature that I liked was the pre-Reformation windows of greenish-white glass; whether this was deliberate or because the art of transparent glass-making was improperly understood is not known, but it looks suitable and somehow fitting.

Framfield's name means Fremma's open land, and the village was not enclosed until 1862, when there were still ancient farms like islands within the waste. This had an effect nationally, for Parliament completely forbade any further enclosures in Sussex in order to reserve the remaining commons for open spaces with a rapidly rising population.

My final thought on this nice little place is that I think it must have a large absent or commuter population, for I never found anyone at home to tell me about their village, each of the several times that I went there.

We move on now from Framfield to Uckfield, which was once a ridge-crest village which has become a small linear town with a truncated railway and a defunct bus station and is now far too crowded to merit long stays. Long ago it had a Bishop's Palace, where King Edward I and his suite once stayed in 1299, when they consumed 82 gallons of beer for which the supplier charged 10/–.

In the Upper High Street are some good buildings, notably the Georgian coaching inn Ye Maidens Head, which I found comfortable; the name seems to date from Elizabeth I having had it renamed by Royal decree from the King's Arms.

An interesting building within a courtyard here has the offices of Dawson, Hart & Co., Solicitors; the firm of which Charles Dawson of Piltdown forgery fame was a partner. It was in Dawson's office that in the summer of 1913 he was surprised by a client who found him staining bones with different liquids, which he explained was to find out how it was 'done in Nature'. But although this may have aroused suspicions, Dawson was a gifted geologist, and for example in 1896 discovered natural gas at Heathfield—it lit the station for many years, until the line was closed in 1964. Dawson actually played a prominent part in the civic affairs of Uckfield being a coroner as well as Clerk to the Magistrates and Urban Council for many years.

The town is left westwards by the B2102 which passes by what used to be an outcrop of Ardingly sandstone called the Rocks; alas it is now completely spoilt by an estate of pretentious two-garage boxes, in contrast to the older and better-landscaped Council houses opposite.

Once away from the bricks and mortar this is a pleasant road down to Shortbridge over the Maresfield Ouse.

Then we approach Piltdown, with its common, golf course and pond, which has a history almost as exciting as, the famous skull, and more authentic. You will see a picture of the skull leering at you from the signboard of the Piltdown Man pub, once known as The Lamb.

For those who may not be aware of him, Piltdown Man held the anthropological stage for over forty years as Darwin's 'Missing Link', even if at times unsteadily, and he was generally accepted as being the earliest inhabitant of Sussex. Briefly, Charles Dawson, an Uckfield solicitor, antiquarian and amateur geologist, found between 1908 and 1915 a skull and other mammal bone fragments in the iron-stained, flint-bearing Pleistocene (Early Ice Age) gravels in a terrace of the river Ouse—which were then unmapped—alongside a farm road leading to Barkham Manor close to Piltdown Common. These were later examined and accepted by Dr (later Sir) Arthur Smith-Woodward, a geologist at the British Museum, and announced to the scientific world in 1912 as a discovery of remote ancestral Man (some 600,000 years ago) and named *Eoanthropus dawsoni* (Dawson's Dawn Man). One famous visitor was Conan Doyle, who whilst he was writing *The Lost World* went at least twice to Piltdown and offered to drive Dawson in his car anywhere he wished. Not everyone accepted *Eoanthropus dawsoni*, and indeed in late 1913 there were suspicions in scientific circles about tampering with the skull and artificial fossilization of the jaw; in 1914 these suspicions actually appeared in print but faded away; and by 1916 Dawson had died.

Piltdown Man was regarded as an 'evolutionary paradox' for in the years that followed discoveries of ancestral man were made in South Africa, Rhodesia and China; and significantly in 1926 when the geologist F. H. Edmonds resurveyed the gravels he found them to be younger than had originally been thought.

In 1953, after careful and prolonged tests using radioactivity and fluorine, Dr Kenneth Oakley of the British Museum announced that Piltdown Man was a forgery. In fact, he was composite: the skull was medieval (1330) and the jaw was from a young orang-utang of AD 1450, and that none of the eighteen finds came from Piltdown anyway. Now, after the initial shock has died down one might expect that nearly thirty years later it would be quietly forgotten; but indeed no, for the mystery of why and who did it is still currently being pursued. One of the reasons is that many famous names were involved behind the scenes, and there existed a certain amount of animosity, jealously and rivalry in both the professional and the amateur scientific world of anthropology. Many books and articles have been written with theories, suspicions and accusations, but none with a complete account of what happened. However, if Dawson was the forger he was not alone in the plot, and in fact he may himself have been duped, but who the undoubted genius was who did it is still a mystery.

Some writers have tried to pin suspicion on Professor Teilhard de Chardin, the famous French palaeontologist and Jesuit philosopher, who as a young priest and amateur geologist was helping Dawson, and who in August 1913 found the all-important canine tooth which was crucial to the fact that the jaw was human. But Teilhard's movements are known in detail

from his letters to his family in Puy de Dôme in France; in
October he was back in France, and in 1914 in the Front Line,
and he did not return to England for many years. Later he was
involved in the discovery of Peking Man, and his subsequent
career points to him being completely innocent of involvement
in the forgery.

There is a photograph in existence which shows all three
(Dawson, Smith-Woodward and Teilhard) working on the site,
and it is possible that whoever took this photograph is the
mysterious unknown forger.

The final thought about the forgery is why choose Piltdown?
Nearly all the river gravels of Sussex have no fossils, and since
Dawson was a competent geologist he should have realized—as
he did—that it was a very rare happening to find any fossils at
all in such an unlikely place.

In 1912 Piltdown was described as a quiet corner of Sussex,
but seventy years later it is a noisy main-road village of little
charm, except for some older houses. One of these is the
medieval farmhouse Moses Farm, the home of James Arched, a
retired farmer. He helped me go back in time by seeking out
Gilbert Grover of Grover's Farm on the edge of the golf course,
and from this I learnt a little about Dawson, whom he remembered, but in between I learnt a lot about the fascinating history
of the golf course.

Piltdown pond, fed from a small tributary of the Ouse, was on
common land, part of which had rather mysteriously become a
nine-hole golf course. This was within the land of the Lord of the
Manor of Barkham, Sir George Maryon-Wilson, Chairman of
the Board of Conservators of Ashdown Forest. Earlier he had
objected to some local villagers using a canoe on the pond, but
they had refused to come ashore when ordered to do so.

In the hot and dry summer of 1921 the pond had dried out and
Mr Grover, as was customary, began to plough out the reeds and
flags, the pond being near his farm. This action was strongly
objected to by the golf club, although at the same time six men
were cutting litter (heather) on the common as a Commoner's
right. In fact some local people had rights of common on
Ashdown Forest, and at one time turned out horned stock and
two hundred sheep for grazing; but of late usage had declined
because of the distance. Mr Grover also used to plough a furrow

to separate the land of the two landowners: Gage and Maryon-Wilson.

The burning question was that the golf club wished to extend their course, and did not want interference on the common. Mr Grover defied their warning and continued to plough out the pond, choosing an early Sunday morning. But the golf club captain had got the police to restrain him, for he was also towing trees out of the pond with an old Army lorry. The pond of course had been important to the village as a water supply, which was not unusual in rural Sussex then; in fact he had remembered his father taking water round to the villagers by cart for a small charge.

Grover seems then to have gone off as a young man to Australia in 1923, where he worked on a 120,000-acre sheep station living, as he told me, on mutton and tea. He returned to Piltdown on a visit, but his father persuaded him to stay and work the farm. It was some time afterwards that he embarked on a five-year litigation and Chancery suit against the golf club. His Brighton lawyer continually warned him that he would lose out and that it would cost him a great deal of money. But he was stubborn and at length the golf club gave in. An agreement was reached which cost him £45 (no small sum then) but he reckoned it was well worth it.

I then broached the subject of Dawson and the Piltdown forgery. The villagers, said Grover, had thought it was one of Dawson's pranks, and although the Kenwards of Barkham Manor had believed it, there was, he said, general laughter about its validity. This rather confirms that Dawson was not held locally in the high esteem that he was nationally.

Westwards from Piltdown where the A272 crosses the Ouse is Goldbridge Farm where on the river banks are earthworks and vestiges of the ill-fated Ouse Navigation in the first half of the nineteenth century. Piltdown even had an inn nearby called the Horse and Barge.

Just to the north of Piltdown lies Fletching, a very different village altogether. The name is a personal one again—the people of Flecci, ing, ingas—a folk name which is fairly common in Sussex and usually means a later settled place. But here the village is quite old for it is mentioned in Domesday, which many of the places in the area are not, although their names may be old.

Fletching's church tower of iron-stained Tilgate stone is early Norman with two narrow bell openings separated by a pillar. Inside the church among the many memorials are one to Richard Leeche, ironmaster (1596), and one to Edward Gibbon, the historian and friend of the 1st Earl of Sheffield.

Outside, it is worth standing next to the fine eighteenth-century Church Farmhouse beside the church. Here you will see good examples of the true Sussex vernacular buildings with the Horsham Slab roofs of the church nave and porch, and the stone, bricks and hung tiles of the farmhouse.

The main street is full of good buildings also, with two pubs, The Griffin and The Rose and Crown, plus timber-framed cottages like the fifteenth-century Dalehamore. Names are interesting too. Some of the houses are called after saints, and two cottages near the top are named after battles, Minden and Naseby. Down at the bottom is an impressive, but not very old, gateway into Sheffield Park.

I walked down the steep little side road to the Ouse where there was once a Tudor forge owned by Lord Buckhurst and worked by Richard Leeche—who had been such a great benefactor to Fletching and to his own Kentish village of Smeethe. The forge site had become a grist mill, still going in 1930s, but apart from the name Mill Farm there was no trace of either. Such are the rapid changes of the last few decades after many centuries of slow, almost timeless growth. But rivers still flood, change or no, and a reminder here was the long raised causeway.

Over the Ouse and we pass Fletching Common, once over 1,000 acres, where Simon de Montfort camped with his army before he gained victory at Lewes in 1216. There is a nice little walk along the river here to Sheffield Bridge, and not far away is the southern terminus of the Bluebell Railway.

The story of this highly enterprising little line, saved from oblivion by a group of enthusiasts and indeed benefactors, has often been told. They now have twenty-eight steam locomotives and some 315,000 passenger journeys a year, but they need to expand and link up with a now very co-operative British Rail; but opposition to this idea seems to come from a small group of people whose reasons are weak but whose powers are great. We shall return to the Bluebell Line in the next chapter when we come to Horsted Keynes and see what their chances are worth in this hostile quarter.

The name Sheffield, which was probably a vill in Edward III's time with numerous taxpayers, is derived from O.E. *sceap* (sheep), an open clearing and later field—which became Scifelle, then Schiffeld.

Up the main road on the right is Sheffield Park. The estate manor is old and was owned by Simon de Montfort, by Henry VI, and twice by the de la Warrs. Then in 1769 it was bought from them by John Baker Holroyd who became 1st Earl of Sheffield and was a rather remarkable character. A Yorkshireman, he fought in Germany as a cavalry officer, travelled throughout Europe where he met Edward Gibbon (who wrote *Decline and Fall*), afterwards becoming a rich man through inheritance, he married and developed his estate as a model farm. He then fought a violent election at Coventry in 1780 where the two city sheriffs landed up in Newgate, inherited an Irish peerage, and later he had the unique position of being two Lord Sheffields— one here in Sussex and the other in Yorkshire. He was an enthusiastic Commoner on Ashdown Forest where he sent his special light-footed oxen to cut many loads of litter.

The family became great patrons of cricket, and a series of three matches were played in their grounds in 1827 with Sussex against All England, with the famous Lillywhite and Broadbridge.

The 2nd Earl was a director of the London Brighton & South Coast Railway and instrumental in building the Bluebell Line from East Grinstead to Lewes in 1882. The 3rd Earl was himself a good cricketer and the patron of modern Sussex cricket. He took a famous team to Australia in 1891–2, and really started the modern Test Matches. The Australians always used to begin their tour of England with a match at Sheffield Park, and the Australian states still play for the Sheffield Shield. In the hard winter of 1890 a game was played on one of the park lakes with well-known Sussex players on both sides and special trains ran to Sheffield Park Station.

The large house is really an early Gothic building completely rebuilt in 1775 round a much older double quadrangle Elizabethan house, and then battlemented. Inside are some very fine animal paintings of lions, tigers and cheetahs by C.

Cotton, R.A., and rare books, weapons and some of Dickens's letters.

The huge grounds cover 142 acres with five lakes. But these were rather different when first laid out by 'Capability' Brown, who made the waterfalls and used a tributary of the Ouse from Sheffield Forest; and Repton landscaped them with trees and shrubs. The 3rd Earl added two further lakes, but the real architect of the present gardens was Arthur Gilstrap-Soames, who bought the property when the Sheffield family died out in 1909. It was he who added azaleas and rhododendrons, which give such a burst of colour in May, and then in autumn come the bright contrasts of the Tupelo tree which starts with scarlet and gold then becomes deep red, the russet of the maples and the many rare conifers like the golden larch which becomes gold, orange and then brown.

In 1952 came the sale of the Sheffield estate, and there were fears for its future, but it is once again in private hands with the National Trust as guardians, but not without a financial struggle followed by generous bequests.

Before leaving Sheffield Park we touch once more on the Piltdown forgery, for Dawson claimed that he had found a cranial bone and mammal bones here in a ploughed field in the same Ouse terrace gravels in 1915. But the actual site was never known—only the field. One of the bones found here is indeed genuine, that of a rhinoceros, but the chances are that it came from the Red Crag of East Anglia not Sussex!

From Sheffield Park southwards and once more over the Ouse, then along the main road for a short distance and down a lane on the right, and before you is a splendid building. This is Wapsbourne Farm, now separated from the farm itself which is run by a company. The house stands on an early moated site (1197), the name of which has no less than thirty-nine variations, all meaning 'way leading to a stress', meaning in turn an alluvial plain by the river easily ploughed.

This farm was part of the Sheffield Manor lands and sold by John Baker Holroyd in 1769. The present house dates from 1606 and is Elizabethan E-shaped with three storeys, partly timber-framed and partly vitreous brickwork, and now owned by Major Lancaster, a cousin of Osbert, the famous cartoonist.

I was very kindly shown over the house by Mrs Lancaster,

accompanied by her handsome chocolate labrador, Bruno. It is a truly fascinating building of nooks and crannies, with a fine glassed door from the dining-room leading on to the lawn.

One can leave Wapsbourne by a footpath which passes through some woods on the slopes above the river to a side road and thus reach Freshfield, whose name presents no mystery being from O.E. *fersc*—fresh or clean. There was a Tudor forge here, which according to Straker has left no clue, but fifty years later Mr Tebbutt, our Forest archaeologist, has found slag downstream, and discovered in an old lease of water rights at the time of Elizabeth I that an earlier mill had to release water to the forge.

There are two bridges here, one over the Ouse and one over the old canal, and looking over the old canal leat and peering up at the signboard of the Sloop Inn it is surprising to realize that just over a century ago there were barges passing here. From the inn no doubt came the noise and clatter of cheerful watersiders and bargees quenching their thirst, but today whilst perhaps on a warm evening you are sitting outside doing the same you might hear the sound of peacocks calling, for a neighbouring farmer here breeds them. Upstream beyond the alder-fringed banks is the old sluice gate of the former canal, and a relic of its once navigable channel.

The history of the River Ouse is complex both in its physique and its different names. We have to go back to the Flandrian Transgression 5,000 years ago when the main rivers along the South Coast were drowned by the advancing sea, and until well after Roman times the lower Ouse looked like the present Langstone and Portsmouth Harbours. The original Celtic name was Midwyn, which referred to only the upper and middle course, meaning 'middle winding river'. The lower course, a broad inlet, was constantly shifting and had no fixed name, at first called Saforda, and then water of Lewes—after the chief town on its banks.

The present name Ouse was not mentioned until 1612, and may descend from O.E. *wase*, itself from Frisian, then M.E. *wos* = ooze (mud); or it may be from Aqua de Lewes, Aqua del Owes—Ouse; or again from French, *eaux* (Oze), waters.

The main channel of the river itself, like the name, did not become stabilized until well after medieval times through

silting, reclamation and dyking. Then in 1790 the Upper Ouse
Navigation Act was passed and the river canalized up as far as
Upper Ryelands Bridge, beyond where the present Brighton
railway line crosses the river. There were eighteen locks, and
seven barges worked upstream; and as we have seen mills and
waterside inns came into existence. The last barge worked
upstream to Sheffield Bridge in 1868.

The inn here was built in 1833, and let into the brickwork of
the wall is the builder's or bricklayer's (probably one and the
same) name: James Parker, August 26th. It remains a more
substantial legacy of a short bygone era of river navigation,
which perhaps one day—when we are satiated with our choked
roads—we might be glad to revive.

5

The Western Slopes

The western fringes of Ashdown Forest slope away gradually in a series of parallel wooded ridges running north to south, and although the main Eastbourne road is a boundary for part of the way, the north-western slopes of Ashdown merge into the surrounding country without any real distinctiveness.

From Wych Cross on the Forest a side road runs westwards past Hindleap Warren to Goats Cross Roads, then through West Hoathly to Turners Hill. Here it joins the old coach road to Brighton (B210) and continues south-west to Whitely Hill on the B2036. The exploration of the western slopes can begin along this fairly level ridge road from which you can at times enjoy really fine views over the Sussex Weald for it was an old prehistoric highway. It also happens to be the watershed dividing the south-draining Ouse from the north-draining Medway, whose source is close to Turners Hill.

After passing Old Plawhatch Hall at one of the old entrances to the Forest we are now beyond the medieval pale. At first there is little change, but then the open landscape gives way to enclosed woodlands although the geology remains similar for the sands of the Ashdown Beds extend well westwards.

The whole area to the south of us is a series of sub-parallel headstreams of the River Ouse, the main river of the Forest Ridges, and these are often parallel with the modern side roads because they are the descendants of the old Roman iron ways and Saxon droving roads in an area of the High Weald that was colonized later by the South Saxons. In fact, it is a landscape of ridges rather than of valleys.

The ridge road from Ashdown continues through the dull suburbanized village of Sharpthorne and the first place of interest is the village of West Hoathly (accent on 'lye'). This was a western outpost of Ashdown, and is an old clearing in the forested Weald, O.E. *leah, ly*—a forest glade or clearing.

There are some good buildings here: the Manor House with its Horsham Stone slabbed roof and the church built in Tilgate Stone—that often beautiful iron-stained limey sandstone from the Wadhurst Clay which has a distinctive russet colour. The church was gradually enlarged over the centuries from its compact Norman building, and is well placed in the middle of the village. Behind there are broad sweeping views from the churchyard over the Ouse basin, with below us one of its headstreams flowing swiftly down a steeply wooded ghyll.

Modern West Hoathly seems to have problems like aircraft noise, and recently a Parish Council survey showed that some of the older people have complained about poor bus services and lack of alternative transport. This set me thinking that it is a pity they were so mute when they were younger over the closure of the railway, which became defunct more than twenty years ago.

Onwards to Selsfield Common, 568 feet up and a nice open spot, where a smock windmill once stood, and where nearly 2,000 years ago the Roman road from London to the coast crossed at its highest point. Still standing not far away is Selsfield House with an impressive early Georgian stone façade, and then comes Withy Pitts Farm behind which was a pond supposed by many people to be the source of the Ouse; but I am afraid it is not, only one of its many headstreams.

Next is Turners Hill, a cross-roads village on the ridge, and just round the corner on the East Grinstead Road is a group of the Cowdray estate cottages, built about sixty years ago by Sir Aston Webb. They are timber framed, stone and with Tudor-type brick chimneys, nicely set back from the road with a statue in the façade of the middle one—altogether a very pleasing group. The church tower by the same architect was not quite so successful, being squat and heavy, but both his works are better to look at than some of the newer houses in the village, although compensation can be obtained in the village inns with which Turners Hill is well supplied.

Out from the village along the old coach road, B2110, we go westwards and soon can be seen some of the finest views in Sussex; from here it is not hard to visualize the great spread of forest that the South Saxon pioneer farmer would have seen whilst he was hacking and clearing his little patch of ground. These splendid vistas were enjoyed earlier by the old Cowdray estate whose impressive 1870 mansion, Paddockhurst, is now part of Worth Abbey School.

At Whitely Hill we are on the edge of Worth Forest, which is a remaining fragment of the old Saxon Andredsweald, before turning and going down the side road by South Hill. There is a long gradual descent through Paddockhurst Park, and then in open country opposite Stony Lane, a road leads down to Little Strudgate Farm and a reedy, tree-fringed lake. From here if you are energetic there is a good walk through to Wakehurst Place at Ardingly.

Opposite the farm is a stone house built in 1901 with the Cowdray Arms on its façade, with a later addition of hung tiles at the back. It fits its surroundings very well, and once again one is reminded that siting is all important with houses; something the modern builder ignores mainly because what he builds is dictated by economy, with so many of the additions to modern farms in pleasant rural areas becoming stark and intrusive instead of harmonizing.

From Little Strudgate, via Stony Lane and the busy B2036, you can reach Balcombe, south of Worth Forest, and a very old site, for the remains of Mesolithic nomadic dwellings have been found here. This is a village which springs surprises on one for at first it appears rather plain, but near the Half Moon pub (a good place to pause) there are some very fine houses. Just two are mentioned here, but they are ones which should be typical of any Sussex village. The first I saw was a modern clapboard house with a Regency bow window with leaded sills, expensive I suppose, but not for those who have decided that economy is outweighed by a pleasing appearance. The other was quite different for it was one of a group clustered around a small green. It was called Alley Cottage and its splendid colourful cottage garden was the best of what used to be so typical of the English village scene. A further joy is to walk down past Balcombe House, where the fine east window with its two wings looks out over to a grand view of the large lake in the grounds.

Before going eastwards from Balcombe a diversion down a side road ought to be taken to see the Ouse Viaduct, which is a very fine example of early Victorian railway engineering. The architect was David Mocatta and he built some elegant little Italianate bridge houses at each end of this long bridge which crosses such a small river. All the stone and bricks were brought here by the river from Lewes by barge for the Ouse was still navigable at the time. In my study I have a large framed photograph taken over fifty years ago of the old Southern Belle Pullman crossing the bridge, and it is a very good aid to nostalgia.

Today the viaduct carries a far heavier weight of traffic than ever the early L.B.S.C.R. engineers could have envisaged, for there are trains crossing every few minutes on a busy route.

Back to Balcombe and down to the mill on the Ardingly road with its cottages in a waterside setting, which with the trees surrounding the now flooded valley for a reservoir makes it look more like Scotland than Sussex.

Further along the road past the house called Lullings the reservoir is wider and flatter, and not so well suited to the landscape, but as if to make up for it there is the Loder Valley Wealden Reserve for the botanical preservation of Wealden vegetation, controlled by Kew Gardens, which is worth the sacrifice of the footpath.

Onwards down the steep hill over the Ardingly Brook and up again crossing the line of the old Roman road, and we are abreast of Ardingly Church, which is half a mile westwards from the village. Its name is derived from *Eardinga leage*, the clearing of Earda's people, this being an early penetration by the South Saxons for their swine pastures, but like many places in this district it does not appear as a settlement until much later.

The church of St Peter is a compact fourteenth-century sandstone building standing at the crossing of two very ancient roads, the first from Lindfield to Balcombe and the other the Roman road we have just passed. Inside the church, which is very much devoted to Wakehersts and Culpepers with many brasses, the impression is one of worship and cleanliness (and comfort, on account of the tartan carpets and beautiful tapestry hassocks) as well as a rare atmosphere of peace—not always found in many churches.

Here I went off down the church lane to seek the old Ardingly forge on the one-time Loder stream, but alas! forgetting that the reservoir has submerged whatever has remained of it. Here it is all boats, fishermen and a rather dreary dam. My wrath rose; are we so wasteful of water that we have continually to impound these rare and isolated valleys in the Weald?

The main things of interest in Ardingly after the church seem to be on the outskirts; southwards lies the 1870 College of the Woodward Foundation, an imposing red-brick building in whose grounds were discovered fairly recently the Tudor iron furnace, companion to the now sunken forge remains; this still has its pond in water and remains of the bay and spillway are about a quarter of a mile from the Loder valley reservoir. Just southwards was Ardingly Station, quite convenient for the school if not for the village. There is a mineral line with a private siding which uses it for roadstone cartage and has a depot at the station.

Northwards from the village along the B2028 on the left is the South of England Showground, and just beyond are the gardens of Wakehurst Place, very fine indeed, but noted more for the harmonious mixture of trees, shrubs, water, rocks and part wilderness than just for flowers. These gardens were pioneered from 1903 by Gerald Loder, 1st Lord Wakehurst.

The house was built in 1590 by Sir Edward Culpeper whose ancestor had acquired the estate in the typical Culpeper manner by carrying off and later marrying one of the Wakehurst heiresses so carelessly looked after by their guardian, another Culpeper, Sir John, his brother. It was altered in 1845 and part demolished, but it is still a very fine building with vernacular materials like Horsham Stone roof and Ardingly sandstone, and is now leased to the Ministry of Agriculture through which the gardens are administered by Kew's Director, and the whole is owned by the National Trust—all in all a very suitable arrangement.

North of Wakehurst is perhaps one of the last outposts of true

Wealden wildwood, where on a May afternoon my wife and I had a splendid struggle through tangled woody undergrowth to find the small furnace pond of Chittinglye Manor Farm in Chiddinglye Woods. It was, we thought, a great triumph to find it at last as it had been described by Straker (in *Wealden Iron*) as 'the exquisite little pond, near the celebrated Great upon Little Rock . . .'. It was, however, silted up and weedy; but there was plenty of slag as evidence in the clear stream, which was also full of fish.

Above this dense woodland are immense craggy outcrops of the rock to which the locality gives its name—Ardingly Sandstone—and also of course the huge rock balanced on a smaller one that Straker referred to. This area in May is usually bright with yellow and pink wild azaleas and pink rhododendrons.

Above this again on the top of the plateau are the ramparts of the Philpots Iron Age fort, which we found, but not without difficulty. Ironically this wild enclave of deep Wealden Sussex has the earliest evidence of recorded settlement in a land charter of AD 675 referring to the Welinga Stone—'Stone of the stream dwellers' and the 'clearing of Citta's people'—now Philpots and Chiddinglye Farms.

From the fort we can return via Philpots Farm to West Hoathly, and then go down Cob Lane past Hook Farm Quarry where the local sandstone was once quarried, and up a short lane on the left of Ludwell Farm. This is an interesting name which will recur again at Horsted Keynes; here it is probably derived from Loudwell meaning a noisy spring, and just off the lane in fact is a well. The farm site is old, but the building itself is a renovated farm on the Broadhurst Estate built in stone in the late eighteenth century, when there was a kind of 'mini-agricultural revolution' following the arrival of a new owner of the estate in 1764. Three farms were virtually rebuilt and enlarged, the thatched roofs giving way to Horsham Stone slabbing, the stone being reused from the demolished Broadhurst Manor, their earth floors being properly paved, and the houses' water supply improved.

From Ludwell a footpath leads back to Cob Lane, and then by Holly Farm and over the Ludwell Ghyll to Highbrook in Hammingden Lane. The name here is a reminder again of the early Saxon droving of pigs into the woods for it means Hemele's denn or swine pasture, and unlike so many in Kent it did not become a settlement, merely a farm. Highbrook is a most interesting and curiously scattered little settlement, which you can reach direct from West Hoathly. Its centre is the very fine church of All Saints built in 1884 with a shingled oak broached spire in Early English style.

Here we have an intriguing example of two quite different versions of a church's history, for a fairly recent book asserts that two affluent ladies disagreed with the bigoted Protestant practices at West Hoathly, and decided to build their own church. So I went along to see for myself, and by chance met the churchwarden's husband (a Lancashire man from Bolton); yes, for here the warden is a lady. He was on his way to wind up the church clock, and he took great pleasure in showing me round personally. Then I saw the official history, which stated that the construction was due to the difficulty of parishioners getting to West Hoathly—no doubt the side roads in mid-Victorian times could be pretty miry. At all events, either for reasons of belief or just Wealden mud, it was built by a Mr and Mrs Kirby and a Miss Weguelin; and was conceived as a local church in every way, for all the stone, bricks and tiles came from the Hook Quarry that we passed a while back, and the font was carved from local stone. When I saw the interior, the hassocks were being busily embroidered for the 1984 centenary—with countryside motifs: foxes, cuckoos and pheasants. The church has a western circular window through which twice or perhaps three times a year the sun sends a shaft of light down on to the dove on the altar cloth.

Outside in the churchyard is a sundial and some splendid trees, including a very fine Wellingtonia, and there are good views over the distant wooded ridges which can be seen in comfort from the seat given by a local baker who had baked bread every day for fifty years. The views from a nearby oast kiln are even better. It is a rather unusual building in this area, but perhaps it was an outpost that failed. It is said that the owner of the land here was incensed at the felling of an old oak, but when he beheld his customary view, it had so suddenly improved that he remained silent.

From Highbrook to Horsted Keynes is not far, the station being reached before the village, and now of course the northern

terminus of the well-known Bluebell Line. The station once had
five platforms, and a double electrified line via Ardingly to
Haywards Heath, which functioned until 1963; up till then
there had been a sign which said: 'Change here for the Bluebell
line'. And then the full might of Beeching descended and the
Bluebell Line was left isolated.

However, since 1972 they have been planning to re-establish
the link with London, not via Haywards Heath, but northwards
to East Grinstead six miles away, the nearest B.R. terminus—in
1978 British Rail gave full commercial backing for this link
with Southern Region. But the snag is that a handful of local
landowners and the local Council have decided they do not want
a train service to London. The Bluebell Line is undaunted and a
public inquiry is being held early in 1983 for a planning
application to be considered by a Government Inspector. My
own reaction to all this is that of the railway's motto: 'Floreat
Vapor'—Let steam flourish!

The name Horsted Keynes (pronounced Canes) is itself
unusual in Sussex, being double; the first part meaning a place
where horses were kept, probably a stud, and the second comes
from Normandy. The manor here belonged to William de
Cahanges, which is a town between Vire and Bayeux in the
Calvados Département, and very appropriately this Norman
town is twinned today with Horsted Keynes.

The approach to the village is marked by some very interesting houses. Past the cross-roads from the station and up a
small lane is the farmhouse of Great Oddynes on the Broadhurst
Estate. I have already referred to the rebuilding of these farms,
and here is a real mixture: Horsham slab roof, brick faced with
stone, and a classical portico, but the general effect is very fine
indeed. Just before you reach the village there are two other
very good timber-framed houses opposite each other with the
name Ludwell recurring again: Ludwell and Ludwell Grange.
Ludwell Grange set me a problem, for it must have changed its
name as it seems to have appeared in some books as Pierpoints,
and I spent quite some time looking for a mythical house before I
realized they were one and the same building.

Into the village where there is a nice large green, near a very
good pub called the Green Man, which is full of railwayana.
Amongst the many splendid photographs of past locomotives

and the glories of steam are some early railway company notices. One reads as follows:

Cheshire Lines Railway
These closets are for the convenience of passengers, and not to be used by cabmen, workmen, fish porters and idlers.

The church like the station is on the edge of the village, but not quite so far away, being up a cul-de-sac northwards on rising ground. It stands in a neat and tidy circular churchyard with its typical shingled broached spire pointing skywards. This spire is a particularly graceful example from the thirteenth century built on a very old site, which may be perhaps even pre-Christian and pagan Celtic—as in the case of the Hellingly churchyard further south (the only preserved Celtic burial ground in Sussex) whose shape is similar.

Inside, much of the church of Horsted Keynes is Norman, and there is a recumbent figure of a thirteenth-century knight, thought to be a member of the Cahanges family who had been to the Crusades.

Church records are well-known documents of history, but here in Horsted Keynes there is a bonus with a journal and account book kept from 1655 to 1679 by the Rector, the Reverend Giles Moore. This is interesting as a record of the social history of the times. He started his incumbency in the difficult Cromwellian period, and had to be examined by a Board of Commissioners before he could take office. After this he found the parsonage 'in so ruinous a state, that it cost mee £240, before I could make it fit to dwell in'.

Another entry reads: 'I gave my wyfe 15s. to lay out at St James faire at Lindfield, all which shee spent except 2s.6d which she never returned mee.'

In his glebe he tried to grow hemp, which had been compulsory in Tudor times 'for the better provision of nets for help and furtherance of fishing'. The Rector's attempt failed miserably financially because the cultivation and harvesting was expensive, and later in 1693 the Tudor Acts were repealed. He also reported on the local crops grown, and noted that the amount of wheat grown was very small compared with oats and other grain crops, for wheaten bread was not then the staple food of the bulk of the population. This was pretty general throughout

Sussex in Stuart times, and bread was usually made from maslin: a mixture of wheat and rye, but barley, peas, beans, lupins, and even acorns and beechmast were added. And as the bake ovens were using furze, brushwood or faggots, and as the hearth was only roughly scraped before the dough was put in, it was full of wood ash, and doctors always advised people not to eat the crust. This injunction lasted a long time and indeed eventually became a habit; and I can remember my grandmother's housekeeper still 'cutting the crust' in the 1930s.

Down the lane from the church is a large and beautiful lake where a bridleway crosses over a long chain of them and then runs up the side of some smaller ones along a tributary stream. These were supply ponds for ironworking and later a leat for a mill was constructed. An echo of all this lies over to the west on the West Hoathly road at Cinderhill Farm, the third of the rebuilt farmsteads that I mentioned earlier, for we are now in the Broadhurst estate.

At length up a short drive from the bridleway stands Broadhurst Manor, a very old estate once belonging to the Cahanges (Keynes) family from 1100, the name meaning wide wood, and as mentioned earlier it changed hands in the mid-seventeenth century. One of the results of the new regime was that the farms then had leases with clauses relating to cultivation, and they had to sow temporary grass leys, wheat and institute other improved agricultural practices. Although the house must have been considerably rebuilt, it still looks very old, and one wing has the typical hung tiles of the late seventeenth century.

From Broadhurst one can enter into the heart of the heavily wooded landscape of the western borders of Ashdown Forest. Much of this area has been called the 'wild garden' country of Ardingly, Horsted Keynes and West Hoathly and is due to the enormous number of exotic trees that were planted in the nineteenth and early twentieth centuries. The trees were Wellingtonias, Chile pines, hemlocks, Douglas firs and magnolias, along with rhododendrons and other plants. A curious feature of this hardly ancient spread of trees mixing with the existing hardwoods on the ridges is that it gives a far wilder and older appearance to the landscape than some of the so-called native vegetation of the Weald. Thus the image of the former primeval forest of Anderida is once again brought to mind. This kind of scenery exists through Birchgrove and along the road to Chelwood Gate, where you pass Birch Grove house, the home of Sir Harold Macmillan, who has his name perpetuated in the Harold Macmillan Clump planted on Ashdown Forest near the Isle of Thorns.

Here on the western edge of modern Ashdown, for most of where we have been exploring was within the ancient Ashdown or even older Pevensel Forest, we now turn down the descending main Lewes Road (A275) and come to Danehill, an old name meaning the now familiar 'denn', or pannage clearing in the midst of forested land; but it does not have any connection with Danes, as some people are tempted to assert.

However, although the site is old the modern village is late Victorian and pleasant enough, with a good church well sited on a hillock high up and built in 1892, approached by a very fine avenue of limes. These are branched over, the boughs trained to form a tunnel giving a most effective entrance to the building. Inside the church is rather dark, but the Victorian woodwork is of a very high quality, and there is a very fine all-seasons Queen's Jubilee altar cloth.

From the church southwards a side road leads to Dane Wood of the Forestry Commission, thus avoiding the main road which though very scenic is hideous with noise and speeding traffic, and passes through the wood. Inside there is a pleasant mixture of trees of great variety—ash, alder, chestnut coppice, oaks and conifers. Among the oaks are many minepits which were once dug for iron ore, for we are on Wadhurst Clay. And here I met a most aggressive squirrel, grey naturally (I have not seen a red squirrel in the Weald for many years, you must go to France to see them in any number). This one was up a tree trunk, motionless except for its tail waving furiously. It stared hard at me in a penetrating, angry manner, and I tried hard not to laugh because—like cats—I suppose their sense of humour is not great.

From Danehill a road leads down to Freshfield Crossways, but on the way is a large Victorian mansion called Latchetts, set well back off the road, and typical of the period we talked about earlier for it is surrounded by a splendid 'wild garden', a reminder of the gardens of houses that children so loved in books by Kenneth Grahame like *The Golden Age*.

At Freshfield Crossways in the direction of Freshfield Halt on the Bluebell Line a narrow road turns northwards, and it was along here that I wandered off the highway almost by accident into the woods around Freshfield Lane Brickworks. Inside here was a glorious untidy stretch of wildwood, old coppices, birds, rabbits and wild flowers and everything seemed as though it had been untouched for ages adding to the intense feeling experienced of being unaware of man, his cars, technology and noise—an illusion of course for none of it was very far away, but it seemed so here. From the woods I went into a quarry, which geologically was a disappointment for the noted sections in the various rocks were far too overgrown to tell one from t'other. There was, however, a curious notice saying: 'Pit dangerous, no swimming.' A more unattractive place to bathe, even on the hottest of days, I could not imagine; evidently the jays screeching around me thought so too.

Suddenly I came upon a most unexpected sight, a large excavated pit pond full of bulrushes and water lilies, a remarkable piece of natural beauty in these extensive untidy workings. Near the entrance is a strange little house built of Cuckfield Stone, quarried locally out of the Grinstead Clay, dated 1864, which means the workings are quite old, the original landscape prior to quarrying having long since disappeared.

Before going back to the Freshfield road there is a house called Treemans a little way up on the left. This has a mention in the Rector of Horsted Keynes's account book which we delved into earlier, about tithes payable by Francis Wyatt of Trimmens; and even earlier in Tudor times it was called Trenmontes. The present appearance is as mixed as the names—timber framing, Tudor chimneys, a curious little bell tower, and an ashlar stone wing with large windows—but all entirely harmonious.

Down to the bottom of the road again and under the railway bridge at Freshfield Halt, which must be nowadays one of the smallest halts on a railway anywhere in Britain. We continue on to the village of Lindfield, a delightful place almost engulfed by the urban tide of Haywards Heath, and although at the outer margin of our western fringe it is specially interesting for its connections with Ashdown Forest. It is a very old place indeed being first mentioned in a Saxon document of AD 765, and the name means an open place with lime or linden trees. Here lived Thomas Culpeper, an early Bailiff of the Forest, when it was Lancaster Great Park, and in Henry VIII's time Thomas Henslow of Lindfield was Master of the Game. He was the father of Philip Henslow of Elizabethan theatrical fame with Edward Alleyn at the Rose Theatre in London. And in 1581 Francis Challoner of here killed a stag from the Forest, after a chase that brought him almost home to the village.

A relic found in the roof timbers of the church here was a tussock, or hassock, of coarse grass, used originally by priests before mats or carpets for kneeling—hence the word today (but not to be confused with hassock, the soft sandstone that is between the Ragstone beds in Kent, or with Hassocks, a rather dull place on the Brighton Line where they grow carnations).

Lindfield was one of two places where famous meetings were held to propose the Upper Ouse Navigation; here it was held at the Tiger Inn. The village is full of very fine old houses, and has perhaps the best group example of timber-framing in the whole of the county.

On the way back to Freshfield is East Mascalls, a Hall house that was rebuilt in the great 'modernizing' period of Tudor and later, when the very sooty halls were roofed over or 'lofted'. This was done by building outside chimney stacks often ornamented with ashlar stone, and many roofs were converted by laying on heavy slabs of Horsham Stone. Sometimes this was too much for the roof timbers, which must have creaked and groaned under the strain, and today some of these houses have a sagging ridge due to the weight. Here at East Mascalls this rebuilding was done with great care and taste; and today the house is surrounded by a fine walled garden.

From here we continue right along to Sheffield Green, where standing at the cross-roads with the A275 is the large handsome early eighteenth-century inn, the Sheffield Arms, which rose to some importance as a coaching inn when the turnpike to Lewes was made in 1752. The other famous meeting to propose the Ouse Navigation took place here, under Lord Sheffield; but he later rather unfortunately hindered—by constant amateur interference—the work of the canal engineer, William Smith, the pioneer English geologist.

From the green we keep eastwards for a while, until on the left is a track leading northwards near a stream, a tributary of the Ouse, which takes us up into Sheffield Forest, with a very fine lake and many rocky outcrops of Ardingly sandstone with tors and cliffs, especially in Beechy Wood and Brookers Rough. A lane leads westwards to Furner's Green, a name that has nothing to do with furnaces, but is local from Furner or even Turner. Here one can continue by the path through Sheffield Forest, over the stream again and climb up on its south side, or go via Tanyard Farm and a steep and narrow winding valley road to Colin Godman's Farm.

This is perhaps the most interesting building and site within the whole of our western slopes. Its site was possibly pre-Norman Conquest, and rather mysteriously has its origins in a building that may have been built by Spanish monks. The core of the structure is a medieval Hall house, probably at first entirely of wood, but there have since been an extraordinary variety of alterations of style and rebuilding with the living level of the house being raised. Later in the seventeenth and eighteenth centuries much brick facing was used, but the whole appearance is incredibly harmonious and complete. I first saw it under poor weather conditions when it looked good, but the last time was after an October storm when the clearing showers produced a hard blue sky and bright autumn sun, and the house in the rain-washed air looked timeless.

The grounds are no less interesting with an iron-bearing ridge within the Ashdown sands running across the site, which with the name Kiln Field seems to mean the possibility of an ancient ironworking or bloomery, as yet undiscovered.

The owner and person I particularly wanted to see is Dr Worthington, an environmental scientist and Commoner on Ashdown Forest, with rights to estovers and the grazing (but not riding) of one mill horse; but as he told me wryly there is no longer any mill and being able to ride on the Forest was not a right (even if he had possessed it) he could have used much anyway.

As he had been at one time the Chief Scientist to the Nature Conservancy and was a man with a great deal of practical experience in ecological, conservation and environmental affairs, I thought his ideas on the future of Ashdown Forest might be particularly interesting, from one who, whilst not actually living on the Forest, was certainly of it. He thought that management planning of wild areas was necessary because of public pressure, along with strict conservation in certain areas, and zones of public amenity—and possibly nature trails. Most of this seems reasonable enough, except that I am not in agreement with nature trails. I shall explain why in greater detail in Chapter 10. However, I considered that his opinions were important and interesting.

From here we make our last foray into the deep recesses of the slopes bordering Ashdown, and by going through Pollardsland Wood and past Wilmhurst we can arrive at Bell Lane which runs from Nutley to Fletching.

Along this road are some interesting houses that reflect much of the history of Ashdown Forest. First comes Woolpack Farm, already referred to in Chapter 1 from its old connection with wolves, and reminding me of a very old and curious saying: 'It is better to see a troop of wolves than a fine February.'

Further down are two buildings called Victoria Cottages bearing the Maryon-Wilson crests, and here at No. 1 is an echo of the Piltdown mystery for in 1906 a Mr Burley gave Charles Dawson a skull, brown with age and with its lower jaw missing, at which Dawson is supposed to have said: 'You'll hear more about this, Mr Burley.' This was reported to a Sussex newspaper in January 1954 by Burley's daughter, Mrs Padgham, then living at Cross-in-Hand, and aged thirteen in 1906.

Not far from here is Searles, an old house with a large lake in the grounds belonging at one time to the Maryon-Wilson family. In 1875 Sir Spencer Maryon-Wilson, a Commoner on Ashdown Forest, owned 1,500 acres of land in the county; and in 1881 Sir Percy Maryon-Wilson was one of a notable group of Ashdown Commoners who to defend their fellow Commoners on the Forest—small farmers and humble labourers, some of whom could hardly read or write—pleaded for an injunction against the Lord of the Manor of Duddleswell, Earl de la Warr, to stop him interfering with the Commoners' rights. In 1900 Mr George Maryon-Wilson (later Sir) became Chairman of the Board of Conservators of Ashdown Forest, a post he held for thirty years.

And thus having encircled the Forest, we shall see what manner of a place it was, and why it is unique today, and what its future may be.

6

The making of the Ashdown Landscape

The wilder landscape of Ashdown Forest is in sharp contrast to the quieter countryside of the surrounding High Weald that we have travelled through in the last four chapters, and can surprise visitors seeing it for the first time. This often happens with people from the North, who although used to open moors in Yorkshire and Lancashire find something familiar in beholding Ashdown and at the same time find it unexpected. Indeed, one northern writer has admitted he always thought that south of Stevenage, England consisted of housing estates interspersed with riding stables, kennels and a few sad fields. This it seems to me shows the modern teaching of geography in a poor light; perhaps the computer was not programmed for south of the Thames. Still, the Northerner was pleasantly surprised on encountering Ashdown Forest and its open breezy heights and wide views of distant hills.

However, to understand the present-day landscape of the Forest we need to delve into a little geology, a subject on which Charles Darwin once remarked, 'It is a capital science . . . as it requires nothing but a little reading, thinking and hammering.'

The oldest surface rocks we can see in the Weald are those of the Ashdown Beds from the Lower Cretaceous system, except for a small inlier of older Jurassic Purbeck beds near Battle. These Ashdown Beds are made up of fine-grained sands, sandstones and silts with small amounts of clays, shales and mudstones, but on the Forest they are mainly sandrock which breaks up easily into loose grains; and below these are often pebble beds which means frequently a poor sterile soil. The Ashdown sandstone can be seen in the many small quarries on the Forest which were dug for building stone, for example at Jumper's Town, near Hartfield, and north-east of Gills Lap; this latter quarry is now rather overgrown with wild vegetation and extremely picturesque. Sometimes outcrops of the stone are seen along stream beds, especially near Wych Cross.

About half a mile north-east of Chelwood Vachery the true nature of the poorer Ashdown soils can be seen in the bare gashed ground on slopes, and with great cuts in the plateau surface due to gully erosion after heavy rain. At Broadstone on the open ground sloping northwards, where there is a good view of the Greensand Ridge and the North Downs, very porous friable sand can be found amongst the heather clumps. It is interesting to reflect on the fact that these poor soils did not stop the earlier settlers from carving out small farms and holdings' on the rough land.

There are outcrops of other rocks like the sticky iron-bearing Wadhurst Clay around Forest Lodge and Fairwarp in the south, and also near Crowborough. Some Tunbridge Wells Sands outcrop by faulting south of Fairwarp, where there is an abrupt change of landscape with the land sloping away southwards. These sands are seen again at Dodd's Bank below Nutley and also at Boarshead and Gildridge north of Crowborough.

The Ashdown Sands were first named in 1861 by the geologist F. Drew working on the Wealden Survey, for he saw them spread over a large area and being very thick on Ashdown Forest itself. Nevertheless, if you want to see the very best exposures of the Ashdown Sandstone you must go down to the coast at Ecclesbourne Glen near Hastings, where the cliffs rise up magnificently from the sea.

So, the beginnings of our Ashdown landscape go back a very long time in geological history—some 136 million years in fact—when the Ashdown rocks were first laid down as sands and silts from large rivers flowing down from the north. These rivers formed deltas which grew out into large sheets of fresh water, becoming sometimes a lake and later an arm of the sea which was over what is now Central France.

Rider at Newbridge Splash

Gathering wood, Crowborough, Ashdown Forest

Forest Ranger's cottage
in the snow

The Airman's Grave,
Ashdown Forest

The Wadhurst Clay was deposited further out beyond the delta into deeper water which was at times in the form of lagoons—fresh, brackish and salt. The Tunbridge Wells Sands were laid down like the Ashdown variety but later, when the delta was pushing outwards. All these Wealden rocks were put down on top of a very ancient platform of old, folded rocks from far earlier times.

Then much later in our Earth's history these Wealden rocks themselves were covered over by an enormous mantle of chalk produced from an ancient sea, and eventually folded upwards into a massive dome by a series of convulsive earth movements, the most important being the great 'Alpine Storm' of the Tertiary Era which raised to great heights the mountains of the Alps.

Later came the forces of erosion—sun, wind, rain, frost—which eventually entirely stripped away the chalk from the middle of the Weald and revealed the rocks that are now part of Ashdown Forest. But the great uparched folds remained, making Ashdown today the crest of the inner or High Weald. This reaches 792 feet at Crowborough Beacon, where the great structural arch is known as the Crowborough Anticline.

Drawing much nearer to our own times, the Weald was once again invaded by the sea to isolate Ashdown as part of a central Wealden island with erosion still inexorably going on. Further upheavals of our area took place, and with the sea retreating the primitive ancestor streams of the Medway, Ouse and Rother flowed down the slopes into the Thames and Channel.

The last episodes of sculpturing the landscape were the great Ice Ages in which we are still living. The Weald itself was not glaciated, but the highest parts like Ashdown must have had small snow and ice fields on their tops, with many feet of ground frozen for at least part of the year.

The warmer interglacials brought changes of sea-level as the ice thawed and melted, giving great floods of run-off water from the streams as they tore their way through the saturated landscape, deeply eroding the ground and carving out the steep ravines or ghylls. As these streams flowed outwards from the Forest slopes they were heavily loaded with meltwater carrying masses of sand and silt. You can see the results of this downstream of the Medway at Hartfield and along the Ouse near

Fletching, as well as by the tributary that flows through Buxted. The Medway and Ouse also had gravel deposits, and those of the Ouse near Piltdown (not so easily seen) were the basis of that most extraordinary archaeological hoax of all time, the Piltdown Skull. More spectacular signs of the Ice Ages are just outside the Forest in the form of massive crags and tors of the Ardingly sandstone at West Hoathly and Bowles Rocks near Crowborough. The less common caves in the Ashdown sandstone near Heron's Ghyll are another relic.

And thus the Forest landscape today survives as a remnant of a former forested wilderness and the largest continuous expanse of heathland in Sussex.

Its plant history is as varied as its rock history, but far less is known about some of the earlier vegetation here than in other parts of Britain because pollen evidence in south-east England is slight. However, we do know that around the delta shores of the primeval Wealden lake there was a completely different vegetation from that of today, with primitive conifers like the monkey puzzle (Chile pine), along with ancient palms and waving horsetails in the freshwater swamps.

After that far-off time until the later geological periods we know only fragments. But certainly during the many millions of years of the Tertiary Era the land had a tropical climate, deduced from the plant fossils that were found in the London Clay on the Isle of Sheppey in Kent, like the Nipa palm found today in South-east Asia. These were exotic plants and their condition suggests that they were swept down to the sea by tropical rivers from places within a hundred miles of Sheppey, which would certainly have included ancient Ashdown.

This tropical climate cooled gradually by the time of the late Pliocene period (towards the end of the Tertiary Era) but even so this primitive British flora included such interesting trees as the Japanese umbrella pine, sassafras, walnut, hemlock, silver fir and spruce as well as present native trees like pines, elm, hazel and alder. So we can suppose that some of these trees were growing on a far-off primitive Ashdown.

But all this disappeared completely during the Ice Ages that followed, for in the glacial periods the exposed high ground of the Forest must have endured a very severe sub-Arctic climate like the Tundra today in the north of Canada and Norway.

Frozen hard and snow-covered in the long winters, the short summer brought just a few flowering herbs that included the attractive mountain avens, a few odd dwarf willows and stunted birch.

Then during the warmth of the interglacials conditions were completely changed: some of our familiar trees appeared for the first time, and in the last interglacial before our own—the Ipswichian—the climate really was warm; this was 100,000 years ago in the Old Stone Age. And our first faint clue of life on the Forest appears, for in 1930 an axe of this age was found south-east of Gills Lap.

However, the cold returned once again with the glaciers advancing, and as we began the history of the Wealden Forest in the closing stages of this last glacial period, so the same must apply to Ashdown Forest. Although its early history may be rather different because of its exposed position, its lower water table and coarse sandy soils, it may never have been quite so heavily forested as the thick natural cover of the heavy Weald Clays lower down. The tree-cover nevertheless must have changed with the climate, although lagging behind in time.

This lightly forested vegetation would certainly have existed during the cool pre-Boreal period and the later warmer and drier Boreal, but with the coming of the warm damp Atlantic climate the forest became much thicker and denser for oaks have been found embedded in the peat bogs on Ashdown. This was the time that the alder carrs began to grow in the deep and swampy ghylls. Mosses grew down in Duddleswell, and two species are still found there.

By this time—perhaps some seven and a half millennia back—early Man had come into Ashdown on hunting forays, and so began to influence the plant growth. Research by Mr C. F. Tebbutt has shown that Mesolithic hunters made large clearings by fire and flint axe to improve the grazing for the animals they hunted. And here may well have begun the familiar open heathland with an increase in birch, hazel and heather. Later on, these would have been widened by Neolithic farmers and throughout the prehistoric times of the Bronze and Iron Ages right down to Roman times, so that the vegetation was never again a completely natural growth. However, during the Dark Ages after the Romans left there was everywhere a retreat from the marginal land in the higher part of the Weald, and here high on the Forest would have come the first of the temporary reversions to secondary forest, and in the more isolated parts some wildwood.

One of the attractions of Ashdown Forest is its mixed plant cover resulting from its varied topography—occasional thick woodland, wide tracts of heather moor and bracken, open woodland of oak and birch on the valley slopes and down in the deep ghylls the alder swamps which used to make travel so difficult for man and beast.

So in spite of man's penetration it survived as a natural waste amid the Andredsweald of the South Saxons, although by Domesday the Forest was ringed with small flourishing settlements, and along its edge there was a landscape of small fields and wooded shaws. One example of this is Suntings Farm which was an old farmstead established just outside the later medieval pale along the road from Newbridge Splash to Steppy Lane.

After the coming of the Normans Ashdown was included in the Rape of Pevensey, and the outlying manors were using the Forest for hog pannage from the oaks and beech. By 1268 it was Crown land, and thirty years later much timber, mainly beech, was cut for repairs to Pevensey Castle. This significantly brings into focus the beech, which appears very often in the forestry records. It is a tree which grows well on freely drained and light soils, and although it is often in association with the oak, it will eventually outgrow it in height and its dense foliage shuts out the light and kills off the oak. These soils conditions are common on Ashdown, and for some two hundred years in the early medieval period the climate was warmer than now, so the beech would have become well established. This was especially so in the north around Broadstone Warren, where today there are very many fine mature beech trees.

The warmth did not last, and in the early fourteenth century there was a sudden and very severe climatic shock which produced harvest failure and famine all over Britain, followed by outbreaks of the Black Death, and the Forest was depopulated once again. The result was a second reversion to natural woodland, with dense undergrowth, a favourite habitat for both fallow and roe deer.

In 1372 Ashdown became a Royal Forest (*Silva Regalis*) and

remained so for nearly 300 years. However, it was not left undisturbed and by the early sixteenth century there had been much felling of trees, illegal sheep grazing and grubbing-up of seedlings and young trees by the grazing of other animals. As the gorse was often set on fire the open character began to be maintained; in fact an Elizabethan survey showed that the only really mature trees left were in the South Ward from Nutley to Crowborough. Two other things now appeared to increase heathland and reduce what was left of high forest. The earlier one was the start of Tudor ironworking with the pioneer works at Newbridge, and the later one was in 1550 with the beginning of another climatic downturn, called rather curiously the Little Ice Age.

This cool period would have stimulated the growth of heath, which can adapt to acid soils, intermittent drought and the high winds which were features of the weather from now on. Thus the vegetation of Ashdown changed drastically all through the sixteenth and well into the seventeenth centuries, what with illicit felling, illegal enclosure and poaching—beyond what was reasonable—of underwood and brushwood timber. Of course it was not unnoticed, and in 1540 a Commission tried to remedy things (King Henry VIII himself had expressed concern at the 'great wast and distruction'), but it achieved little, and the decay continued.

With the early Stuarts the woodland recovered and boundary fences were repaired, but at the outbreak of the Civil War the Forest was sequestered and a Commonwealth Commission had some really practical suggestions for afforestation gathered in a massive report, which went the way of all flesh once Charles II was restored. The next thirty years brought complex and acrimonious squabbling between enclosers and Commoners, the outcome of which was yet another Commission. This time, however, their eventual award laid the foundation for the present landscape of the Forest.

Now more than half of the 14,000 acres of Ashdown were enclosed, and a belt of commons created across the Forest's backbone from Chuck Hatch to Duddleswell. Smaller commons were grouped along the edge of the Forest near the villages. One interesting fragment of vegetation was a group of fields near Chelwood Gate surrounded by high slopes of rough heathland called the Isle of Thorns, which had been enclosed in 1564. The name evokes a long-vanished patch of medieval blackthorn woodland and ancient wildwood.

So the Forest became two parts, one of 6,400 acres of common land, part of the Manor of Duddleswell—the Ashdown Forest proper of today. The remainder of over 7,000 acres became private land, although there are some public footpaths which cross these enclosures.

The landscape of these commons has hardly changed in nearly 300 years, apart from encroachments by squatters and the growth of sub-spontaneous Scots pines from planted game coverts. These pines have spread so as to form a band of trees along the edge of the main road between Nutley village and Dodd's Bank. The pine clumps were not liked by Repton, the landscaper, who in 1800 called them 'miserable Scotch firs'.

In complete contrast to the commons the landscapes of the large private estates have changed considerably during the last three centuries, with much tree planting, often conifer plantations acting as 'nurses' for young hardwood trees. Today estates like Crowborough Warren contain mostly Corsican pine, Scots pine and chestnut coppice. Others, such as Five Hundred Acre Wood, still have many fine oaks and beech as a legacy from earlier planting, whilst the largest estate, Pippingford Park, has a much wilder aspect with mixed woodland and open copses, and an attractive chain of lakes which were once used for ironworking but are now the preserve of private fishing.

Many of the smaller enclosures became very fine parks and gardens with many ornamental water features like fountains, lakes and cascades. In the nineteenth century many of these spacious gardens were planted with exotic plants and trees brought from the far corners of the temperate regions of the world like the Caucasus, Himalayan slopes, Japan and Chile.

In 1862 the Reverend Edward Turner of the Sussex Archaeological Society noted that there was much more timber on the Forest: 'Principal timber trees . . . were pine, oak and beech and in some parts were . . . covered with pollarded oaks.'

The landscape was also affected by the activities of people, some of whom were referred to as the 'bonfire boys', both from the Forest itself and from surrounding villages like Hartfield and Withyham, who, it is said, put candles in jam jars and set the open heath on fire—partly just for fun and partly to maintain its open character. Of course grazing their cattle achieved the same result, but more slowly. Nowadays, with grazing in decline, these fires (from whatever cause) are a mixed blessing for they produce gully erosion and destroy plants and the habitats of birds and animals.

But the landscape is changing, albeit in a rather more subtle manner, for on the lower slopes are appearing pioneer gorse and birch (seeds of both are easily spread) which later lead to trees like Scots pine, sessile oaks and even beech. Higher up nearer the crests bracken is invading the once heavily grazed uplands, because the soil drains very freely and the underground rhizomes or root stems of the bracken soon colonize the area. Thus, some of the Forest is in the early stages of returning to a kind of wildwood for the third time since the Dark Ages—perhaps not altogether a bad thing.

Water features are an important element in any landscape, and although they are not very conspicuous, the springs and streams on Ashdown are a distinct part of its countryside. The springs rise from the top of the Ashdown Beds, where the silts outcrop, and as these are more fertile the early farmsteads used these spring lines like the one which lies along the side road today from Newbridge to Chuck Hatch above the Steel Forge river.

Such streams are part of the larger Wealden river system, and have a rather complicated history through the later uplift of the Wealden Island, the rises in sea level and, of course, the ups and downs during the Ice Ages. They were flowing high in the warm interglacials and scoured out their valleys deeply (which were later filled with alluvium, peat, silt and clay swept downstream). Today Ashdown Forest is the most important watershed in the High Weald and divides the headwaters of the Medway flowing northwards to the Thames and North Sea from those of the Ouse flowing southwards into the Channel. This watershed follows the crest of the Crowborough Anticline, and by following the Nutley-Duddleswell road you can almost walk along it.

After the retreat of the glaciers there have been some curious stream diversions. The upper part of the stream, known by its various names—Mill Brook, Three Wards Brook, or the one I

like and use, Steel Forge River—was at one time a headstream
of the River Ouse. For the first two miles of its course it flows
very definitely south-east through Chelwood Vachery and Mill
Wood before it turns abruptly north and flows down through
Mill Brook Bottom, Londonderry Farm, Newbridge and into the
Medway at Withyham. This stream was captured by a powerful
Medway headwater cutting back and diverted into the parent
river. A smaller tributary and Medway headstream has deeply
eroded the side of Camp Hill where it rises and flows down over a
thick slab of Ashdown sandstone, making one of the rare
waterfalls on the Forest, called the Garden of Eden, before
flowing along Old Lodge Bottom. This is a nice little fall after a
storm or heavy rain, but to see it at such a time you have to go
along in wellingtons.

Just outside the Forest there are other stream diversions like
the Heron's Ghyll—a recent stream name—which has lost its
upper headwaters to the stream that flows down through
Crowborough Warren, and one time worked the mill there with
its very chequered history before reaching the lake in Buckhurst Park and joining the Steel Forge River, and thus the
Medway. All this means that generally the Medway is swelling
its catchment at the expense of the Ouse, and so the watershed is
gradually creeping southwards.

Westwards the Kid Brook rises out of Hindleap Warren and
then flows down into Kidbrooke Park, where in more spacious
days it had an adventurous journey through cascades, a canal
and a series of lakes before swelling the Medway at Forest Row.

Rising on the southern slopes of the Forest are two headstreams called the Maresfield Ouse by Straker. It is an interesting reflection on the use made today of streams or even the
interest taken in them that so many are nameless. If they had
names they are long since forgotten, otherwise they seem to be
just anonymous watercourses—which is a pity. Of these two, the
more easterly rises near Nutley and flows down steeply through
a deeply incised valley and then into the large and beautiful
lake at Boringwheel Mill, below which at Cackle Street it is
joined by a short side-stream from Spring Garden which has had
a spirited little journey over the only other waterfall on the
Forest. The main stream then goes on to Old Forge and under
the A22 to Maresfield, where it suddenly is christened and

becomes the Batts Brook. The more westerly rises at Duddleswell and flows by Oldlands and Hendall Manor. The two of them join at Park Farm and so united become the Maresfield Ouse proper and flow into the parent Ouse at Shortbridge.

Over on the west are a whole group of small streams rising below the Wych Cross to Plaw Hatch road that eventually unite and flow into a whole chain of large lakes and ponds above Horsted Keynes before running into the Ouse at Freshfield. There is no shortage of water for all these streams because the Forest has a high rainfall, for Southern England, with 36½ inches at Crowborough Beacon, so they are continuing the age-old process of carving out their valleys which gives for us the pleasing variety of the Ashdown landscape of deeply wooded ravines cut into the soft sandrock.

When we come to look at the soils of the Forest, they never seem to have been anything but rather poor, sterile and mainly sandy and very permeable indeed at the highest part of the Forest. There are differences of course within the landscape of height, aspect and drainage, usually being better in the south. In the north the topsoil becomes heavily leached and washes out the mineral nutrients, leaving a rather dry infertile soil. In fact if you are walking across the open parts of the Forest crests you can sometimes see in a ditch examples of the classic soil type known as a podzol—from the Russian, meaning ash-grey soil (around the 1870s Russian scientists were very active in pioneering attempts to classify soils). This particular one is well named for the top level, or horizon, is pale grey and below it is often a rusty brown layer, from iron-staining, and below that again is the yellowish colour from the Ashdown Sands beneath.

There is no doubt that over the centuries these Ashdown soils have not been helped by the heavy grazing and burning, which has destroyed what little humus or vegetable matter they had. Still, in spite of all this, the early settlers pushed through the Forest rim and carved out their little cultivated patches. In fact they marled these poor soils so thoroughly for long periods, and then worked them, that they actually managed to improve their condition—at any rate for pasture. Some of these old marl pits, which were really clay pits for they were dug in Wadhurst Clay or the seams of clay in the Ashdown Beds, can still be seen pitting the surface of the Forest and often filled with water;

there are still some left near the sites of the old Forest entrances or Gates. Many of these small farms have survived and are there today on the southern slopes at Duddleswell, adding yet another element to the mosaic of this unique landscape.

7

Man on Ashdown—Prehistoric Times to the Great Award of 1693

If you cross the Forest for the first time, which could be on a characteristically grey day with low cloud scudding over the crests, you might well wonder whether anyone in fact had lived there in times long past. And if you are of a historical turn of mind, you might recall William Cobbett's acid description: '. . . a most villainously ugly spot', and later wrote of the 'miserable tracts of heath and fern and bushes and sand . . .' when he compared it with Romney Marsh.

Certainly until comparatively recently it was thought that the first permanent settlers were those in the early Middle Ages, but archaeological field-work and excavation within the last few years has revealed a far more ancient story—not only did prehistoric Man penetrate into the Forest, but it seems that he lived there for quite lengthy periods of time.

In the last chapter there was a brief mention of the discovery of an extremely old artifact near Gills Lap; now, finding one Late Stone Age hand axe does not of course mean that Man actually lived there. Still, it is interesting to consider what might have brought him there 100,000 years ago. The landscape, of course, would not have been quite the same as now, and beyond the fringes of Ashdown there would have been a luxuriant growth of trees for that was the warmest part of an interglacial with larger animals, such as the hippopotamus and elephant which haunted the swampy valley of a primeval

Thames. So it is not stretching the imagination too much to suggest that primitive Stone Age Man was probably attracted to the slopes of Ashdown with its game and rich vegetation to hunt and to make temporary clearing in the natural wilderness.

Man's part in all this is of course speculation (apart from the axe), but the existence of the rich forest and its fauna is not, as paleo-botanists have demonstrated from plant and animal remains found in the sands below Trafalgar Square in London.

So much for this warmth and early Ashdown Man, for there is an enormous time interval between them and the next evidence of Man here. We have come forward now to the times of the post-glacial warmer and drier Boreal climate following the retreat of the glaciers when there was greater expanse of land here than now. Mesolithic (Middle Stone Age) Man some 9–10,000 years ago could have travelled, if he had need to, from Ireland to Germany without getting his feet wet. His presence on Ashdown Forest has been shown by the spread of flint flakes, cores and potboilers, which meant he lived here for at least part of the year, because these seem to have been the relics of hunting expeditions. However, the pioneer discoverer of these finds, Mr Tebbutt, is convinced that there was a certain amount of organized forest clearance. This would have been done by fire or by ring-barking, to widen the area of feeding grounds for the animals that grazed them such as red deer or wild cattle.

These Mesolithic flints were usually used just downhill from the flat ridges, so as to avoid 'dead' ground, and thus the hunters managed to get a much better and longer view of the valley bottom. If you are walking on the Forest you can visit some of these sites and see the views from them—which brought Mr Tebbutt to this conclusion—and this will give added interest to what you are looking at. One viewpoint is from the west side of the Camp Hill pine clump, another is at nearby Stone Hill on a ridge which gives good views to the south-east and a third, which produced an enormous number of flints over a small area, is at Broadstone giving a very fine view northwards of the distant Greensand Ridge and the North Downs.

There is another very remarkable site, but not on public land, on a hill spur known as Garden Hill 550 feet above sea level. This not only has good views nearby but wide sweeping distant vistas of the North and South Downs as well. Some flints were found here in 1972–3, and as we shall see in a moment this site has a long history of occupation from Neolithic to Roman times.

The later Neolithic people, the New Stone Age farmers, probably occupied many of these sites and enlarged them, this time to graze their domestic animals, and in time the wooded area decreased. Bronze Age people also came to Ashdown, perhaps some 2,700 years ago, using arrowheads that were quite different, being barbed and tanged with a sharp point or spike. Only one tool from these early metal workers has been found here, a palstave (axe), which you can see in Brighton Museum.

Something more solid in the shape of evidence can be seen at Peat Lump Hill (close to the 'Four Counties' distance dial), where there is a Bronze Age burial mound which has been robbed at some time.

The last prehistoric people to have lived on the Forest were the Celtic Iron Age miners searching for ironstone, and so we can return to Garden Hill. It was there that round about 100 BC these people built a fortified camp of about 7 acres with a typical entrance set back from the ramparts for safety.

I was shown this very interesting relic of prehistoric Man by Mr Tebbutt, who had found it by chance in 1968 when he was looking for a badger's sett. Having found a badger's latrine on his own land, he asked a neighbouring farmer if he knew where the badger's sett lay. The farmer suggested a likely place would be a small circular wood called Garden Hill; this had never been ploughed and indeed had lain undisturbed for centuries, apart from an old quarry at one edge. Then whilst walking uphill to this wood and looking for the sett, Mr Tebbutt noticed the curious lie of the land around the edge of the wood. With the practised eye of an archaeologist he suddenly realized that he was looking at the ramparts of an old fort. He followed round the ramparts until he reached where the entrance was, large enough in fact for a cart to have entered. Later excavations by another archaeologist, Mr J. H. Money, inside the fort revealed the remains of two round houses, domestic forging hearths and a baking oven, as well as some pottery, making up what seems to have been quite a little industrial unit.

Out on the open Forest again you can see some old earthworks at Gills Lap, that might be Iron Age or perhaps later Roman, with a bank and ditch enclosure, and another group near Chelwood Gate, known as the Danes' Churchyard.

The people who came after the Iron Age Celts to live on Ashdown were quite different, being highly organized and civilized—the Romans. They were not long in realizing the potential of the whole surrounding area for ironworking, for use in London or for export to the Empire. This decision was a landmark in the Forest's history, for not only was this the first organized exploitation of its minerals, but the first metalled roads now appeared on Ashdown—not to be seen again for another 1,400 years with the coming of the Turnpike Trusts.

The Romans removed the old Iron Age defences at Garden Hill and converted it into a small civilian administrative headquarters with the normal amenities of a villa and bath-house. This HQ was designed to organize and co-ordinate their widespread iron industry which operated with many small skilled units over the High Weald and the Forest. You will find further references to this in Chapter 9. Around the slopes of Garden Hill are what appear to be lynchets—the ancient cultivation terraces—so the Romans may have grown corn there as well, which is not unlikely because in the second century AD the climate was warmer; certainly nothing has been cultivated here since.

Looking at Garden Hill now it seems beautifully isolated, but in the Romans' day it was linked by minor roads to the main London to Lewes Way at Gallipot Street in Upper Hartfield. Isolation returned in the third century when the whole unit was abandoned.

This main Roman road, which ran directly from London and across the Forest to Lewes, was built about AD 100, and together with the other Wealden iron roads can be counted as remarkable feats of early road engineering. Of course the Romans were the people who built the road over the Simplon Pass at nearly 7,000 feet—this was not improved upon until Napoleon arrived.

The Roman road across Ashdown was discovered by Ivan Margary from air photographs taken in 1929 at his own expense, which he then followed up by tracing its course with patient and careful field-work along the ground, literally over hill and dale, by means of its raised causeway or agger.

Now, those stalwart walkers interested in combining a

pleasant hike across Ashdown Forest can, with a little amateur archaeology, follow the line of the road. You can still see some traces of agger, metalling and ditches, but unfortunately during the last war tanks using the Forest as a training ground destroyed much of the Roman road's remains.

The road enters the Forest at Chuck Hatch, crosses the B2026 and a small ghyll, a tributary of the Steel Forge River. It then goes through the small isolated enclosure of Lone Oak Hall, where the agger is 18 feet wide, running through a holly grove, and then leaves the enclosure at exactly the south-east corner. Some years ago in wintertime without the bracken it could be seen running up the hillside in open country, but it is rather difficult to see it now.

At the hill crest the road passes about 150 feet from the south-west corner of Five Hundred Acre Wood, and meets the modern long-distance footpath of the Weald Way which has come up from Fisher's Gate and Withyham. Near here was a feature which showed up very clearly on Margary's air photos; this was where the road, eighteen feet wide, was bordered by ditches 62 feet apart, leaving a flat unmetalled space at the side. These were common on the more important roads like Stane Street, except that there they were 83 feet wide, so Margary concluded that 62 feet was a standard width for the Roman secondary road. These widths are astonishing when you realize that most British roads were rather narrow (about 28 feet for the average 'A' class road) until the advent of motorways, in which with their enormous wasteful margins we seem to be copying the Romans. But their wide margins were to avoid ambush.

At this point our stalwart walker has been following the long straight alignment from Edenbridge, which ends just short of the modern B2188 from Groombridge to Maresfield. The Roman road now makes a sharp turn and runs parallel with the B2188 to Camp Hill. You can now follow the line of the Roman road as both climb up along the spine or main ridge of the Forest. The Roman road was arranged so as to go round the heads of the two valleys on opposite sides: westwards to Old Lodge and east-wards to Old Mill House, Crowborough. Soon you are abreast of King's Standing, an historic spot we shall return to later; and the two roads continue on to Beggar's Bush opposite the Radio

Station. Here the Conservators have preserved a section metalled with iron slag (although most of the road was in fact paved with Ashdown sandstone). The notice informs you that the road was built 'in AD 100 shortly after the Romans invaded Britain' ('shortly after' here means fifty-seven years, as the Roman Conquest was in AD 43).

After Camp Hill with its pine clump the line of the Roman road passes through the Duddleswell cross-roads and then straight as an arrow heads for Lewes, going behind Streeter's Farm to Duddleswell. Streeter here may mean 'dweller by the street' from the Roman *strata*—street or road. It reapproaches the modern road, now the B2026, and crosses it about 240 yards north of Fairwarp church where Margary saw agger and slag metalling. A footpath from the church crosses the line of the road in the open Forest; and then the Roman road goes away from Ashdown at Old Workhouse Farm, Fairwarp.

After the Romans left Britain, and probably some time earlier from Ashdown itself, abandoned sites would soon have become overgrown with the tangled secondary forest, effectively concealing the Roman ironworking sites—leaving them for twentieth-century archaeologists to unravel.

So, for some considerable time—perhaps more than two hundred years—during the Dark Ages the Forest was left undisturbed. For a long period the record is bare and, apart from some Saxon coins discovered at Duddleswell in 1820, there was no evidence that the Saxons had ever lived on Ashdown. However, in 1980 a bloomery was discovered near Millbrook Clump in the Mill Brook, or Steel Forge River, valley and was dated at about early ninth century.

By contrast, the surrounding High Weald just outside the Forest was quite well settled by late Saxon times; and by Domesday there were many flourishing settlements carved out of the forested Weald, although they would still be attached to far distant manors, many down on the Sussex coastal plain.

Ashdown Forest, as we know it now, neither existed in name nor boundaries, but rather as a high, partly forested waste surrounded by the wooded Weald, which although cleared in part and settled, still extended north and south into the clay of the Low Weald of Kent and Sussex.

The Normans included it in the Rape of Pevensey which was a

Kidbrooke Park, Forest
Row

Pippingford House in
1869, Pippingford Park

Roman Bloomery with iron slag, Great Cansiron

The Lake, Boringwheel Mill, Ashdown Forest

large area of about 180 square miles attached to Pevensey
Castle and held by Robert, Earl of Mortain, the Conqueror's
half-brother, and the whole forested area was known as
Pevensel.

Now at this point we should examine the custom of Common
Rights, which goes back far beyond Norman times, and also
Norman Manorial Rights and ecclesiastical privileges (abbeys,
priories, churches and chapels) which involved the use of
forested land.

Common Rights are invested in land, not persons; they have
varied over the centuries and from common to common. Some of
them are well known, such as pasturage (to graze stock),
pannage for pigs (beechmast and acorns), and turbary to cut
peat or turf for fuel. But many are lesser known like estovers to
take underwood and pollarded branches for firewood and fences;
housebote to take large pieces of timber for house repair;
haybote (hedgebote) to take thorns or wood for repairing fences;
agistment, or the right to cut herbage; piscary to fish; and finally
one that is a little obscure—heathbote—which it seems was
really a time-honoured custom rather than a right to cut
heather, bracken and the like for the litter. This last was an
important item for the people on the Forest; the word was a
portmanteau expression covering all scythed vegetation like
bracken, heather, furze, gorse and broom. In later years a
special short scythe like a hook came into use for this. Many
centuries later the Ashdown Commoners were to find that litter
cutting was customary and not an actual 'right'.

The Earl of Mortain was not long at Pevensey, being starved
out of his castle by siege, at the instigation, it seems, of William
Rufus who then granted the Pevensel Forest privileges of
pannage, housebote, agistment and estovers to the Abbey of
Grestein in Normandy.

Even by Plantagenet times we do not know how large the area
was which we now call Ashdown Forest, nor indeed are we
certain of the origin of the name, whose earliest form seems to
have been Hessedon, in about 1200. By 1275 this had become
Hassedon or Ashdown, suggesting that it was from O.E. Aescen
(Ashy) referring to a down or upland area (dun) which was
covered with ash trees. However, these trees are rare on the
Forest (the acid sandy soils are not to their liking; they prefer

damp limestone soils, which is why ash trees are so common in the North of England in Carboniferous Limestone country where they often form complete woods). It is much more likely that the name is a personal one from Aesc or Aesca's dun (Aesca's hill).

By the time of Henry I (1100–35) Pevensey Castle and its forest had been granted to Gilbert d'Aquila, and in 1229 in Henry III's reign (1216–72) d'Aquila's great-grandson founded the Priory of Michelham in the Cuckmere valley near Hailsham. As usual, this was a large endowment, including not only Pevensel Park, but also lands and tenants in Maresfield, Hartfield and Cowden (Kent). The Priory's privileges in Pevensel Park were mainly pasturage, but the Rector and Chaplain of Maresfield seem to have had much wider ones—pannage, housebote, haybote, heathbote and firebote—all apparently supervised by the Master of the Forest.

The Priory's connection then with Ashdown Forest was important and long lasting for they held the Vachery for over four centuries until it was bought by Daniel Rogers in 1650. Incidentally this priory at Michelham is one of the best-preserved buildings in Sussex and was at one time owned by two of the great Sussex families, the Pelhams and later the Sackvilles, who owned it from 1603 to 1897. One of their tenants in the nineteenth century was the celebrated breeder of Sussex cattle, Thomas Child, and the building today is reputed to be haunted by quite famous ghosts!

Returning to Pevensel Park, it is interesting to note that a medieval 'park' meant simply an area of over 30 acres surrounded by a bank or pale, to keep deer from straying out or in; and this is the first evidence we have that Ashdown may have been enclosed or emparked. We still do not know how large it was, but certainly it must have been far larger than today. The word 'park', used so widely nowadays for all manner of things, comes from O.E. *pearruc*, which is a diminutive (like bull-bullock) from the old Germanic *Spar*, a beam, from *sparren*, to enclose, lock or fasten. *Pearruc* became paddock, and park(c) is the French form of the spelling—complicated but intriguing!

These common rights of the local free tenants existed by tradition and ancient practice rather than by any form of codified law, and as the Normans were organized people and liked to have things written down rather than know them by vague word of mouth, it is not surprising that sometimes these practices were questioned. This happened in 1245 when the Chief Forester of the 'Honour' (or seignory of several manors under one lord) of Pevensey investigated timber that had been felled in the forest, for no doubt more than a reasonable amount had been filched, and probably now begins the long history of stealing wood from Ashdown. This may have been one of the reasons for the forest area being invested in the crown (Henry III) in 1268, and the Manor of Duddleswell being held direct by the King. Matters must have been sorted out, for by 1273 in the new King's reign (Edward I, 1272–1307) the 208 customary tenants on the Forest edge were allowed to take estovers. They paid 39½d rent and most paid in kind—208 hens at Christmas and 416 eggs at Easter, the medieval custom being to date these events by Church festivals, like Hocktide, the second Sunday after Easter. This little transaction gives an idea of medieval money values.

The other neighbouring manors were quite restricted in their rights, which were pasturage, herbage and pannage, although the tenants of the two Royal manors, Maresfield and Duddleswell, as well as those who had houses on the Forest, could also take estovers.

In the last chapter I referred to the thick beech forest covering Ashdown at about this time; this is borne out by the existence of a large swine population, which in 1297 was 2,123 hogs (swine for pork) and 557 pigs (young boars and sows), on the Forest. Beech must have been in good supply by 1298 for much wood, which was mainly beech, was taken from Maresfield Park and Essedoun (Ashdown) Forest for repairs to Pevensey Castle. Fifteen years later, Queen Margaret, the wife of Edward II (1307–27) and who then held Pevensey, allowed Robert de Sapy a hundred oaks for repairs, once again to the castle.

All this must seem to us now to be a lot of wood, but anyone who has ever seen Pevensey Castle—first the enormous area of the Roman fortress of Anderida which covered 10 acres and whose walls are in good condition even today, and then the very large Norman castle with a moat, three towers, keep and gatehouse inside the Roman walls—will realize that its upkeep must have been enormous. Even in 1940 the castle's defensive role was not over, for the towers were reinforced and the keep covered with disguised pill-boxes against a possible German invasion!

We have now reached the fourteenth century which for England was full of dramatic events; two have passed firmly into history books, the other has been ignored. Those that are well known are the two outbreaks of the Black Death in 1348 and 1350 and the Peasants' Revolt in 1381. What has been ignored was the sudden severe downturn in the climate, which resulted in drenching summers and famine in the years 1314 to 1325, and undoubtedly laid the foundation for the other two events later in the century; all three must have affected life on Ashdown Forest.

Edward II built a hunting lodge on Ashdown, and a popular tradition amongst writers has been to place it in many different places, the favourite being north-west of Nutley, at Chelwood Vachery. This lodge was in Maresfield parish, which also had a free chapel built inside a wood half a mile west of Nutley, today known as Chapel Wood. This chapel fell out of use in 1541, for a chalice and vestments were transferred to Maresfield church; this small event may be significant for it was during the Reformation, troubled times for the Church.

At all events the chapel survived longer than the hunting lodge, for its walls were still there in the eighteenth century, and its font was discovered in 1800 beneath the earth, only to be lost once more and found again fifty years later, being used for a cattle trough!

We have some clue as to the size of the Forest in 1324 when King Edward at Withyham ordered that some proceedings against Tunbridge foresters should be stopped. The foresters would have been from the old South Frithe Forest which stretched far beyond where now Tunbridge Wells lies—probably not far from the River Medway, which was then the northern limit of Ashdown Forest. One estimate for medieval times has put the size at 15,000 acres, but if the strip along the river frontage is included it is more likely to have been 18,000.

It was in this century that a new form of woodland village evolved; this was the waste edge settlement. Along the edge of Ashdown three had grown up. One of the earliest in the north was the rather formless hamlet of Coleman's Hatch with its cottages sited near springs on the silts of the Ashdown Beds. Another was at Forest Row, then called Walhill Hatch and first mentioned in 1338 as just a single street of houses. The most interesting was Nutley, whose name comes from Knutu Leah, a nut tree in a forest glade or clearing, which was recorded as early as 1249. By 1291 it had become Notley, and by 1333 Nuttely, when the settlement was a series of farms and small-holdings carved out of the Forest. These settlements were no doubt originally encouraged by the warm medieval climate which had spread tillage far up into the hills in Southern England. On Dartmoor, remains of thirteenth-century corn-drying ovens have been found at 1,200 feet up.

However, in 1362 the foresters' records show a deterioration in the climate for a fierce gale caused much loss of trees, including many beech in 'Assedoun' Forest.

In 1372 came one of the great landmarks in the history of the Forest, for Edward III (1327–77) granted 'the Forest of Ashdon' which was a 'free chase' (an unenclosed hunting ground) to his third son, John of Gaunt, Duke of Lancaster. And for the next three centuries it was to be a Royal Forest (*Silva Regalis*) known as Lancaster Great Park. John of Gaunt, amongst his vast possessions, already had a deer park at King's Somborne in Hampshire. This was tiny in comparison with Lancaster Great Park, for it was less than 400 acres, but it contained the valley of the River Test and its tributary the Somborne with their important fish stews or ponds. What we do know was the economic function of Somborne Park, which would have been very similar to Lancaster. This involved the killing of all the winter meat at Martinmas (11th November), which was cut into strips (collops), salted and then stored. The breeding stock was turned out on to the common lands where they led a rather grim, half-starved existence in the winter months.

Lancaster Great Park was enclosed, as was customary, by a deer-leap fence. This was an earth bank four to five feet high topped with wooden palings or stakes, plus a deep ditch on the Forest side and a bank sloping inwards to the fields. This made it difficult for the deer to break into the farmland, but if they did manage it, they were able to leap out again. The fence, or Pale, was broken here and there by gates into the Forest called hatches. These were high half-wickets with an open space above crossed by a high bar which prevented the deer leaping through. This word hatch, a local Sussex name, is from the O.E. *haecc*, itself from an old Germanic word *xak*, of unknown origin.

Within the Pale were some copyholders (tenants) of the Royal Manor of Duddleswell, who had their small commoner holdings—little closes dug by spade—and who protected the King's interests; and outside the Pale were a few freeholders with commons rights. This medieval Pale can still be traced in some places around the perimeter of the Forest today, although much of it was destroyed by enclosures made in the late seventeenth century. However, you can still take a pleasant walk eastwards from Legsheath Farm on the north-west boundary of the Forest, where the original bank and ditch still exist between what were the medieval gates of Lagsheath and Malles. The walk begins through a very fine beechwood, which later changes to rather spindly birches, with some hornbeams and large oak trees giving a nice selection of the variety of woodland to be found on the Forest.

Some of the hatch names have been preserved in place-names such as Prickett's Hatch along the Piltdown road south of Nutley. This name has a variable origin, for it could come from pricket, a young deer, or from pricker, a forester; if it is the latter then it might mean forester's entrance gate, which sounds logical enough. There are two small hamlets on the northern edge, one already referred to and the other being called Chuck Hatch, which also is slightly controversial as to its exact origin. If indeed it is 'chuck', it may mean a gate near where chucks or blocks of wood were cut and hung to make the gate self-closing; but if it is 'churk', as in Churkenhatchgate in 1564, then it meant a 'churking' or creaking gate!

On the eastern side of the Forest there are two other survivals: Fisher's Gate and Friar's Gate. Needless to say neither has anything to do with fish or monasteries! In Cromwell's time they were 'Fidges gate and frayes gate'. The first is from Fitchett, an old word meaning polecat, and Frayes is probably a person's name, for it had become Frayes Gate by 1795. Finally Plawhatch, which today survives in house names, comes from O.E. *plega*—play or amusement. And here is a most amusing coincidence, for the elegant Victorian mansion of Plawhatch Hall built in 1875 and set amid exotic gardens has now become the property of First Trade Union Country Club, to give its full name—I leave it to the reader's imagination to guess what sort of 'play or amusement' happens there.

John of Gaunt's possession of Ashdown lasted twenty-seven years, for he died at Leicester in 1399, and one of his later acts had been to bestow the chapelry referred to earlier on his heretical friend John Wyclif. This was in keeping with his strong character for his interests were spread far and wide, from Scotland to Portugal and Calais. The Great Park now reverted to the Crown and much of its later history is marked by a long decline in its vegetation. However, in medieval times foresters' lodges were built down in the deep valleys, where they cultivated some land, preserved trees for the browsing of deer, and made sure there was plenty of vegetation to act as coverts such as wild raspberry and blackberry. The sites of these lodges later had large houses built on them when the Forest was partially enclosed in the seventeenth century, and the names still remain: Old, New and Hindleap Lodges.

The Park in the three centuries of its existence changed from a medieval hunting forest into an Elizabethan deer park with standings, or bowers, and later on to a Jacobean one with hunting towers and deer cotes. The only relic of all this activity is the well-known viewpoint of King's Standing where the Old Lodge Road (B2026) meets the road from Groombridge (B2188).

This place is an old site, and air photographs had revealed what seemed to be quite large square earthwork enclosures of about 19 acres. These were excavated by Ivan Margary who found all manner of things: bricks, tiles and red medieval pottery; going down deeper he found signs of Roman and prehistoric occupation. The name itself is not so old, as in 1693 it had been called Kinge Stand and later in 1813 King James's Stand. Margary realized the site was of long occupation, and thought it might have been a medieval hunting look-out. Mr Tebbutt, our Ashdown archaeologist, thought that perhaps there might be more to discover, so he delved into the history of deer-hunting since medieval times to find out the history of the site.

Medieval hunting was a very robust and extremely tough affair, usually involving a single stag (red deer) or buck (fallow deer). This animal was pursued by hunters and hounds through forests, across streams, and over rough ground, until it was brought to bay and killed by hand at dangerously close quarters. However, it seems that the later Tudor and Stuart monarchs preferred to hunt in an easier fashion, especially Henry VIII and Queen Elizabeth I who in their later years were not exactly mobile enough to hunt with the hounds. So hides, or standings, were used; these were hidden raised platforms from which the deer were shot by longbow or crossbow, and later arquebuses were used. But the quarry had first to be decoyed by a tame or 'call' deer into an enclosure leading to a standing. It appears that James I (or at any rate Jacobean gentlemen) used the place later with a more substantial hunting tower built of bricks and tiles. 'Lightlands', the Tudor ironmasters' house south of Frant, was often used by royalty after they had hunted on the Forest (they reached the building by a long bridleway via Hazelhurst).

Mention of decoy animals reminds me of the time when I worked in Argentina, and was visiting one of the large frozen meat works, or *frigorificos*, at La Plata near Buenos Aires. Here I saw under a large tree along with some horses and grazing contentedly some fat cattle and a particularly prosperous-looking sheep. These I learnt were decoys for the slaughterhouse, and were always referred to as *animales traidores*—traitor animals—by the meat packers.

Hunting the royal deer was but one of the activities within the Forest, as the Commoners were prone to poaching game, killing deer, thieving horses and destroying woodland. The Royal staff were not above these malpractices either, probably caused by that age-old social ill—absentee landlords and distant impersonal administration. This had come about by a change in status, for although the earlier Forest Bailiffs had lived and worked on the Forest, the post later had become one of high social standing and the holders no longer lived in Sussex. The later administration was carried out by a Master of the Forest with a staff of rangers and verderers, and another post which also later became hereditary—Master of the Game. In fact, the last local holder was Thomas Henlow of Lindfield in Henry VIII's reign (1509–47).

Of course abuses of the Royal Forest were of long standing, for quite early in its history, in Henry V's reign (1413–22), John Pelham, then holder of Pevensey Castle and its manors and lands, had been charged in 1418 with (amongst other things) waste by sale and destruction of timber in Ashdown Forest and Maresfield. Much later in Henry VIII's time at a Forest Court held at Nutley in 1519 there was a whole catalogue of complaints by Commoners against foresters not only for taking and selling timber, but grazing their own stock during the close season for deer-hunting and allowing hogs and large numbers of cattle belonging to strangers outside the Forest to graze within the Forest—not without profit, one suspects.

An interesting late medieval practice which continued for some time afterwards was that of rabbit warrening. The warrens, called 'pillow mounds', were long banks of earth enclosed by ditches and a perimeter bank. They have given distinctive features and names to the Forest topography, such as Broadstone, Pippingford, Prestridge, and Crowborough Warrens. You can still see some of them, one at Northbank Wood and another in Broadstone Warren. That historic spot, Garden Hill, also had one, then called Gardine Hill in Hartfield parish.

In 1540 a Commission was set up at Henry VIII's instigation, as I mentioned in the last chapter, to gather information about the state of the woodland, poaching of game and deer, and the state of the boundary fences. It is worth quoting what they thought of Ashdown Forest: '[it] is a barren ground and hathe no covert of any underwood saving greāt trees . . . there is no faire launde in it but only hethes and they are not playne but all holtes.' Here 'barren' does not necessarily mean 'bare', and 'holtes' means wooded copses. This Commission's effects were nominal, and their decisions are not known.

The troubles continued in Mary Tudor's reign (1553–8): poaching, as well as marauding deer damaging land beyond the Forest, having been disturbed by organized gangs from outside like the one from Hartfield. The gangs used crossbows and greyhounds, plus a fearsome array of other weapons, and under cover of darkness attacked and wounded keepers, and killed red and fallow deer.

In 1564 during the early Elizabethan period a complete survey of the Forest was made, and it was noted that there were now 158 acres of land held by Copyholders within the Pale, and 242 acres without the Pale. Those holdings beyond the Pale had vastly increased, mainly at Crowborough, where there were a great many small-holdings, thus heralding the growth of that extraordinary piecemeal town. It is interesting to note that the name Brown's Brook is first mentioned in the survey; in the earlier report of 1540 it had been Brown's Lodge so its origin is either a person, or the colour of a stream.

We can see that by the sixteenth century the old Royal Forest was changing through a conflict of interests—those of the iron-master, grazier and encroaching farmer—a process made easier as the boundary fences were broken down, and not repaired, as the Royal hunting declined.

When we look back from the late twentieth century to this time, we should perhaps be aware of not just Ashdown, or even Sussex, but an England that was thinly populated—at the most perhaps 3 million—not even three-quarters of the total for Roman Britain. Communications of any kind were slow; important matters went at the speed of a messenger on a fast horse, or for any distance by relays. Otherwise it was by word of mouth for everyday affairs. They had been much faster in the old Roman Empire, when a message could reach Rome from Britain within thirty-six hours!

The seventeenth century opened with yet another Commission, this time requested in 1605 by the Master of the Game, Thomas Sackville, Earl of Dorset, for repairing fences to preserve the game, and to sort out the tangled web of ancient grazing rights. The inquiry operated from Duddleswell, where the Sackvilles had a lodge as their official place of residence on the Forest; as a building it has not survived, although the foundations can still be traced and a piece of window mullion has been found. The common rights of the free tenants of both Duddleswell and Maresfield Manors, and the limited rights of other tenants, were noted. Pasturage and estovers were acknowledged for a number of people on the western fringes—over a hundred for example in Fletching, thirty-two in East Grinstead, the remainder in West Hoathly and Horsted Keynes.

Some definite improvements resulted, but in general the Crown was lax about its property. Crown sales began under James I (1603–25) and continued under Charles I, who in 1640 sold a large amount of land in small plots and patches on the fringes of the old Deer Park at Crowborough, which later became the property of expensive house builders. The agents of the Crown, rangers and keepers, still enjoyed a number of privileges; usually the keeper's lodge had 20 acres of land around it, and the Head Ranger owned considerable property and exercised great power. One such was Sir Henry Compton, who built Brambletye House in 1632, having taken the stone from a building known as the White House on the Forest; he had already taken some from the old Buckhurst mansion, but as he was married to the daughter of a Sackville (Robert, 2nd Earl of Dorset) one supposes nothing was said or done about it.

Then came the Civil War and the Commonwealth, and the disturbed state of the nation was reflected in renewed outbreaks of deer-poaching and illicit felling of trees. The situation was not helped by Parliament's 1651 Acts of Disafforestation applying to all manors and forests and restricting common rights on former Crown Land.

However, in 1650 the Commonwealth Parliament, realizing the possible value of the Forest, made a complete survey which amongst other things evaluated the six great medieval walks and their lodges on the Forest. The largest, Whitedeane of 1,856 acres, was worth an annual rent of £150, although it had no timber; the most valuable was Broadstone of 1,145 acres worth £250 and its timber £80; and the smaller Pressridge of only 417 acres had timber worth £120 and its rent only £73. The whole Forest was worth £2,300 for its 14,000 acres—a substantial sum in those times. Incidentally, the Sackvilles (Earls of Dorset) did not come out of this survey very well. The Earl was accused by the Commissioners of holding a number of properties including Buckhurst Park and Newnham Park (just north of Heron's Ghyll) without any real title to them, as they said his ancestors had enclosed them illegally. His grants given by Charles I on the Forest of timber, fish ponds, forges and furnaces were also declared void—rather naturally one would suppose!

The values of land and timber on the Forest and its peculiar use, which to the Commonwealth Parliament probably seemed inefficient, must have influenced the first of the two great Commissions made in the second half of the seventeenth century. This was in 1658 by the Commonwealth, making a really genuine effort to deal with the problems of land owner- ship in the former Deer Park, and to examine the customs, rights and uses of the Forest. A particularly well-drawn scheme of enclosures, which suggested fresh land ownership, was devised by Adam Moore with a total of 4,462 acres of common land for the claims of the 2,746 cattle. However, with the restoration of Charles II the whole carefully documented report vanished into the State archives, and the gay period of Merrie England began.

On the Forest began a new era of enclosures with the disappearance of the old Royal Forest. Earlier in 1658 there had been many small enclosed plots at Nutley beyond the Pale. In the year of the Restoration (1660) another one was at Sweet Minepits, just south of the Duddleswell road; this was a relic of ironworking on the Forest, and has since been renamed Marlpits.

The Earl of Dorset now reappears on the scene. He had asked for and obtained an appointment as 'Master of the Forest' on the grounds that his ancestors had held the appointment in fact, though not in name, and he paid a nominal £5 per year for this privilege.

But in the next year the Earl of Bristol was granted the lease of the Forest for 99 years at a rent of £200 per annum. This caused friction with the Earl of Dorset, who apparently then agreed to receive £100 per annum. This arrangement did not last long, for in 1664 it was leased again to Sir Thomas Williams, who became Lord of the Manor of Duddleswell (originally a Crown Manor), and held this position for the next thirty-five years.

There was some talk of re-establishing the Deer Park, but times had changed, and enclosure of waste land and improvement by farming were now great sources of profit. Therefore some of the land was divided up and sown with corn and grass, and although this seemed an outrage to some of the Commoners' traditional grazing rights on the open heath, it was in some respects the faint beginning of land improvement and agricultural revolution to come. You can see some of these original enclosure banks today from Old Lodge to Duddleswell Lodge, and from Wych Cross to Coleman's Hatch.

Land was later sold to private owners and two well-known estates came into being: in the 1660s Pippingford Park was bought by the William Newnham whom we came across earlier at Maresfield; he planted trees as coverts for blackcock game. The other estate was next to Buckhurst Park, was bought by Symon Smith in 1678 and is known today as Five Hundred Acre Wood. This last estate was thought at the time to be a nice example of Restoration 'back-scratching' as Smith had helped Sir Thomas Williams earlier to get Ashdown. Later it was acquired by the Dukes of Dorset. There were many other smaller holdings enclosed—forty-five in all—at two shillings per acre, in contrast to the few pence of earlier times.

These land transactions caused great resentment amongst the Commoners, so much so that they smashed the fences and trampled down the growing corn on the wide-open expanse of heath where the farms and fenced plantations had encroached on to 'their commons'. But some of them were 'tenants by custom', as squatters were called, and nothing like the amount of common land the Commoners claimed had in fact ever been commons; in 1680 they had been initially offered 5,000 acres which they had said was not enough.

This inevitably led to a great lawsuit in 1689 between the Earl of Dorset, now the owner of Five Hundred Acre Wood next to his Buckhurst Park property, and his lessees, against John Newnham of Nutley and other Commoners. The Duchy Court where the case was heard decided that an independent Commission should divide the Forest into private enclosed land and sufficient grazing land for the Commoners of the surrounding hamlets and villages. So we approach the next great landmark in the history of Ashdown Forest—the Commissioners' Award of 1693.

8

Man on Ashdown
the Aftermath of 1693 on the Forest

After two years of carefully collecting evidence the Enclosure
Commissioners made their final award in 1693, and so a landscape was created by a legal document that in many ways has
remained static for nearly three hundred years. This relatively
unchanged feature is the large belt of common land over the
centre of the Forest from southwards near Fairwarp through
Duddleswell northwards to Chuck Hatch, with an offshoot
north-west to Wych Cross. This pattern was created to leave the
private enclosed lands within the remoter centre of the Forest,
as there had been many suggestions that any 'improvements'
should be confined to that part.

Then a series of small commons was made around the rim
based upon the repeated pleadings that the waste edge of
Ashdown should not be enclosed or improved. So the present
shape of the Forest evolved from the extreme south at Lower
Horney Gate north-westwards through Nutley to the extreme
west at Lagsheath Gate; then north-eastwards to Kidbrooke
Gate and east and south-east through Quabrook Gate to
Newbridge, east again to Chuck Hatch, round Friar's Gate
through Crowborough St John's and southwards by Oldlands
Gate—a total of 6,676 acres that was thought enough for the
Commoners' grazings.

This meant that of the total of nearly 14,000 acres more than
half was enclosed; and the main private estates are now in a

wide band down the middle of the Forest. The largest awards
were as follows: Pippingford and Old Lodge, 2,175 acres; next
was Crowborough Warren of 1,425 acres, followed by Hindleap
Warren of 588 acres and then Prestridge Warren of 306 acres.
They tailed off after that into many small parcels—some of
which were rather complicated—and an interesting small
award was Kidbrooke of 33 acres and odd amounts like those on
Broadstone Walk where Widow Thompsett got 1½ acres. Her
name is commemorated today in Thomsett's Bank by a small
stream that runs into the Medway east of Forest Row, along
which are patches of gravel dating from the Ice Ages.

Two Fermors—a real Sussex name this, although originally
from Picardy in France in the reign of Edward III—Richard and
John got five and eight acres each, and the Shelley Arms Inn (an
earlier one) managed to acquire just over an acre at Nutley. Nor
were some of the earlier 'tenants by custom', or squatters,
forgotten for their allotments at Highgate, north of Forest Row,
were confirmed, and a considerable area of land, some 900 acres,
in small sporadic parcels was ring-fenced at Duddleswell and
enclosed, mainly for Sir Robert Clayton, including many places
familiar today as Brown's Brook and Fairwarp; the latter was
the lodge of the large house at Oldlands. Many of the freeholdings here were held by tenants living outside the old Pale at
Coleman's Hatch and Newbridge. It was not surprising after
these awards to find that there was much dealing in land, the
leading parties being Alexander Staples, father and son, who
obtained Sweet Minepits and had 2½ acres at Londonderry.

Some people actually lost land, like Isaac Snelling, who had to
forfeit 116 acres, but he had been busy earlier in what was
referred to as 'opening out'; this was land obtained by some very
doubtful and shady dealings. The Commoners, of course, now
lost their ancient rights of pasturage, herbage and pannage on
the newly enclosed lands, but out in the open commons of the
heathland they had the sole right to pasturage, which at that
time did not normally include sheep. Probably the reason for
this is simply that sheep graze the turf too closely.

Not even the Lord of the Manor, as owner of the soil, had
grazing rights, but later he did have the privilege of cutting
litter. For the Commoners, estovers were limited to birch, alder
and willow, but this was not always so carefully observed, for in

more modern times residents of East Grinstead took timber like oak, maple and whitebeam from land near Nutley.

From 1693 onwards the history of the former Royal Forest of Ashdown is in two distinct parts—public and private—and as separate as a train being divided at a junction.

Ashdown Forest from now on generally means the commons, that is distinct from the private enclosed land. From 1699 the Commoners settled down under a new Lord of the Manor, Jacob Hooper, and later in 1720 John Crawford. And as the record is bare for this period, one supposes that it was a fairly peaceful one. Then in 1730 the Lord of the Manor passed to the Sackvilles, now the 1st Duke of Dorset, whose ancestral home at Withyham we passed by earlier in the book. There were to be many future quarrels between the Sackvilles and the Commoners, but for the moment things were quiet, and it was in a completely different way that the open spaces of the Forest were to be disturbed by law breakers, and this was not just the popular pastime of poaching blackcock game and rabbits. This was, in a word, smuggling. Because it involved not only the Forest for quite some time, but also places on its fringes like Hartfield, Copthorne in Surrey and Groombridge in Kent, and the nearby assize town of East Grinstead where the smugglers were often tried, it is as well perhaps to delve into history to find its origins.

The real beginnings of smuggling in England were the illegal exporters of wool known as owlers. This had come about in the Middle Ages by the great influence of the Clothiers, a powerful pressure group and large employers, who had depressed the price of wool on the home market. They had strongly opposed the sheep farmer exporting his wool crop, and no less a person than Geoffrey Chaucer in the fourteenth century was a form of Customs officer who helped to suppress the 'trade'—and on occasion pocketed the fines imposed!

In Tudor times it was cannon that was being smuggled (a subject for the next chapter) and by the eighteenth century smuggling had evolved into a vast professional network, and as Daniel Defoe put it, 'the reigning commerce of the English coast from the Thames to Land's End'. What is more, it involved the whole of society, gentry, squire, parson, farmer and cottager, who were ready to buy the illegal imports and, for often very different reasons, discreetly turned a very blind eye to what were sometimes rather nasty crimes committed by the smugglers.

Now, smuggling has been romanticized by many famous authors such as Georgette Heyer, Rudyard Kipling and Russell Thorndike; and indeed there was much that *was* exciting and romantic in it. Plenty of secret passages, moonlight rides, clandestine signals to offshore ships in the dead of night, secret rendezvous with innkeepers and buyers and a whole lot of risky and no doubt dangerous activities. The only unromantic element was the smuggler himself, who was often a violent, notoriously tough, cruel and insolent character who would browbeat and threaten informers or unlucky accidental witnesses with death if there was the slightest chance of his activities becoming known.

In 1745 the Government reduced the duty on tea from 4/9 to 1/–, which instead of improving matters only made the smugglers more active than ever for they now concentrated on high-value spirits like cognac and gin.

Hawkhurst was a cross-roads village in Kent and one of the main centres for 'run' goods which passed from here by two routes. The first was cross-country via Uckfield to Petersfield, Petworth, Midhurst into Hampshire and Dorset, and the other was northwards via Groombridge—incredibly long distances for those days, and very well organized. Both Hawkhurst and Groombridge were the centres of notoriously ferocious gangs who operated over very wide areas of country.

Now where Ashdown Forest came into the picture was as a very conveniently isolated and rough area for the temporary or longer periods for storing goods in secret caches or hiding places. There were no lack of these on the Forest, with a number of isolated farms and cottages in places like Duddleswell, or a farmstead down in Cackle Street (on the way to Oldlands from Courtland Gate); both these areas were the haunts of smugglers and poachers. Also, apart from the natural hollows found in the Ardingly sandstone (which outcrops around the extreme south of the Forest like Dodd's Bank, Courtlands and a cave at Lampool and in the grounds of what is now the Doma Farm Nursery), there were many small quarries and plenty of pits which had once been dug for iron ore and marl and which could be used. And as the Forest in the 1760s was regarded as 'bleak and barren as moorland in Yorkshire and Westmoreland', its natural vegetation was useful for hiding goods like the famous Beggar's Bush, a large clump of holly trees north of Camp Hill cross-roads; its name, traditionally, comes from a dead beggar found there. And finally for real isolation there were the unfrequented swampy alder carrs with their thick tangled undergrowth.

There were many routes or hollow ways across the Forest, and in 1747 John Kelton produced his famous map of Lancaster Great Park which showed some of these ancient 'horse roads'. One in particular was the way from East Grinstead to Rotherfield, which came into the Forest at High Gate, near Forest Row, and then went via Broadstone Ground, Pippingford Warren, Crowborough Warren and out of the Forest at Heave Gate south of Crowborough.

One of the most ancient was the packhorse trail used for centuries from Duddleswell via Camp Hill to Nutley. Over the years these hollow ways had been churned up by horses' hooves and gradually widened into many parallel tracks; a situation that is happening too today with rather different types of horse riders, who apparently are sometimes using them illegally, like the smugglers did. However, most of the old users were probably genuine travellers and traders.

Smuggling reached its peak in the years 1747–8 when it was estimated that there were some 20,000 engaged in this 'free trade' with 500 alone at Hawkhurst. Of course some were caught, but not with much help from the inhabitants of the Forest and its fringes, who themselves had a reputation as poachers and horse thieves! There was always, too, the ever-present fear of the smugglers' revenge which was far too gruesome for most honest folk to inform on them.

However, when they were caught they often appeared in the Assize Court at East Grinstead, as did some of the famous Hawkhurst Gang in early 1747: Lawrence and Thomas Kemp, John Smoaker Mill and Francis Doe, along with some famous highway robbers like Jockey Brown, although—as far as the judge was concerned—there was little to choose, to paraphrase Dr Johnson, 'between a louse and a flea'. (Incidentally, later on Johnson was *not* well disposed towards smugglers.)

Usually notorious smugglers were sent for trial to London because impartial juries were non-existent in Kent and Sussex. But even with the break-up of the infamous Hawkhurst Gang in 1747 at the Old Bailey trial smuggling continued, although much more intermittently. In October 1783 Buxted villagers saw a large packhorse team openly escorted by armed sailors who had been convoying their 'run' goods to Ashdown Forest. These sailors or 'sea smugglers' were usually such competent seamen, that if caught they were immediately drafted into the Navy instead of being hanged.

Gradually the authorities got on top of the situation, but more through the methods of 'dog eat dog', such as were used by Walter of Horsham, who had a troop of well-trained excisemen. They nosed out the secret hiding places, and had many successes like the huge haul of brandy near East Grinstead in 1781. Walter apparently made a good thing out of excise work, for he was reputed to earn £5,000 a year, an enormous sum two hundred years ago.

About this time the new Turnpike Trust was building roads over or near the Forest. The East Grinstead-Uckfield road is mentioned in the opening chapter, but in 1766 three more were built locally. One road was from Tunbridge Wells through Crowborough, with a turnpike at Crowborough Beacon, to Uckfield—the forerunner of the present A26; another was across the Forest from Groombridge to King's Standing, with a turnpike at Duddleswell Crossroads, and thence to Maresfield. Long dykes were built on either side at Duddleswell to prevent vehicles from driving over the Forest to avoid the toll; and sometimes it was thought that these dykes were the remains of something more ancient. This Groombridge-Maresfield road is now the B2026 and B2188. A third was built from East Grinstead to Tunbridge Wells, the forerunner of the present A264, although for some years it was considered a secondary road and numbered B2110.

These roads were newly built, for the old hollow ways were deeply sunk lanes, difficult to metal and often meandered like rivers. On the Forest the old Roman road with its splendid road-bed was also left, probably because by this time it was covered over by centuries of disuse; indeed it was discovered only from the air by Ivan Margary in the 1930s. However, later

many of the roads were metalled with Roman slag found at old
bloomeries, particularly the one at Oldlands in Maresfield
parish.

In 1793 the people of Ashdown were excited to see a great
parade of troops on the Forest with twelve regiments of the
British Army having a huge camp between Duddleswell and
Nutley. Years after they had left some curious low circular
mounds were discovered in the area; these puzzled archaeologists, until Ivan Margary concluded that they were the
remains of the soldiers' field kitchens.

Two years later in 1795 the long smouldering disputes
between the Commoners and the Dukes of Dorset burst into
flame with a lawsuit over the cutting of litter: heather, bracken,
broom, gorse and rough grass. The Duke thought that this
would remove the cover for game such as the blackcock—a bird
that has long since departed from Ashdown, its nearest habitat
now being Dartmoor—and that the shooting would be ruined.
The result was, as the Duke won his case, the planting of clumps
of Scots pine as cover in the form of small reservations, which
further infuriated the Commoners who met in protest to throw
down these new enclosures.

Of course all the local farmers cut litter, in particular the 1st
Earl of Sheffield, whom we met earlier. He used his specially
bred light oxen, much more sure-footed in the Wealden mud,
and fetched as many as forty to fifty loads a year for his well-run
farm estate.

This litter-cutting seems to have been a perennial source of
argument on Ashdown, and later the Commoners were to
discover to their cost that it was really only a custom, rather
than an ancient right.

However, in the meantime they met at Nutley and in 1816
decided to make proper reservations where no litter would be
cut; these were made at King's Standing, Gills Lap, Five
Hundred Acre Wood, Crow's Nest, Hollies Down near
Broadstone, and Giggs Bush near Pippingford Park entrance.

Gills Lap, perhaps the most famous landmark on the Forest
today, has quite a history for its site was once called Boyletts
Boyes; Gills Lap, or Jills Lap, was a knoll 160 yards south of the
present road fork between Kidds Hill and the B2026. It was
planted in 1816, when the other clumps were planted, but since

then it has had other names, one being Deal Mount (Dial Post as at West Grinstead on the Worthing Road, A24) on an early nineteenth-century map. In this sense it is appropriate to refer to the 'Four Counties' distance dial only a few yards along the road southwards.

In 1940 some people referred to it as the Camel, Camel's Clump or the Maresfield Camel (as one inhabitant of Edenbridge called it). This was because at that time two of its trees seemed from a distance to be shaped like a camel, and this was seen clearly both from the Withyham–Motts Mill road and the railway between Ashurst and Groombridge. Before the last war there were fifty-seven pine trees in this clump but in 1940 there was much cutting down, and one local historian, Father Philip Malden of Heron's Ghyll, said he hoped that the Conservators would keep the camel's contours—well, readers, go up and see for yourselves if this is so.

But Gills Lap was also the scene of murder in the late eighteenth century, with a miraculous intervention on the part of a witness to save an innocent and pious young apprentice who had, it appears, been unjustly accused. The apprentice, whose master was an unscrupulous tradesman in Tunbridge Wells, was bullied for his piety, and they were on rather bad terms. One day master and apprentice set out to transact some business at the Crow and Gate Inn on the Crowborough road. Afterwards they parted, the master to collect some rents from Chuck Hatch, and the apprentice to walk back to Tunbridge Wells via Rotherfield where he had some business. There was no one at home in Rotherfield, so he completed his walk back to Tunbridge Wells without meeting anyone that he knew; but a stranger asked him the time when he was at Redgate Mill. The apprentice told him that he would soon hear Rotherfield Church clock striking four o'clock, which it did.

Meanwhile the master had been attacked and murdered by unknown assailants near Gills Lap. The apprentice was later arrested for murder and committed to Lewes Assizes. His alibi being unsupported testimony, the outlook was black in the extreme for him.

On the night before the Assizes a farmer living at Great-upon-Little Farm, West Hoathly (named after the famous rock there which we passed in Chapter 5; the farm is now either

Chiddinglye or Philpots), was sleeping when he thought he heard a voice telling him to go to Lewes; thinking it was a dream he ignored the 'message', but it was so persistent that in the end he got up and saddled his horse and went to Lewes, arriving in time for breakfast at the White Hart there. He did not know about the Assizes, but when told went and got a seat in the Public Gallery. In due course the apprentice's case came up, and he related his simple defence regarding meeting the stranger at Redgate Mill. On hearing this the farmer got to his feet and told the judge that he wanted to give evidence. This he did, and the apprentice was duly acquitted. The story is considered entirely true, and appeared in a Lewes paper at the time, and later was published in a book.

There were still problems on the Forest, however, as some of the small Commoners were really only scratching a living from their little holdings, and grazing their stock on the rough wild pasture of heathland, although at this time there was little improved pasture anywhere in the High Weald. These Commoners were still probably better off than many of the landless labourers in the surrounding villages in the grim decade from 1820 to 1830. One illegal activity was that people other than Commoners were cutting peat, and grazing their stock—peat of course was in great demand for fuel.

The upshot of all this was a famous meeting of some Commoners including noble lords like Biddulph of Brambletye and Cavendish at Walkhill with the young Lord of the Manor, Earl de la Warr (the Dukes of Dorset succession had lapsed, and the female line continued through the marriage of a Sackville to Wests, the de la Warr family). This meeting was held at the "Maiden's Head" Inn, Uckfield, in 1830, with other Commoners like Lord Sheffield and old Lady Shelley of Maresfield Park. They decided to control illegal cutting of litter, and as the damage done by removal of turf and peat was so bad, they instituted a ticket allowance system for the local poor which lasted for another 55 years, until all turf and peat cutting became illegal in 1885. A reminder of this activity is in Nutley, where Clockhouse Lane was once called Turfstack Lane, and there is a Turfstack Cottage there.

The only real village on the Forest, Nutley, did not have a church until 1845. This is small with a high roof in Early

English style; an aisle was added in 1871, and the whole impression is that of a pleasant little building.

The only other village on the Forest is Fairwarp, a rather modern place that seems to have grown from a single farmhouse built in 1777 on a track across the Forest, later to be called Rose Cottage. At all events an infants school was opened in 1873, described as a school 'on the Forest' rather than Fairwarp. There were then a dozen houses; and a church was built in 1881, the parish being carved out of Buxted.

As the church has a long connection with Oldlands Hall and estate, at this point the history of this interesting area immediately beyond the present south-western boundary of the Forest is relevant to our story. Oldlands, said to mean the 'old ironworking lands' of Roman times, was the traditional name of the valley and land now covered by Oldlands Wood. In an old document of 1219 Oldlands appears as 'Eldelond', which was about the time of the revival of thirteenth-century medieval ironworking, so that former places worked by the Romans were described thus. On the estate is a sixteenth-century farmhouse which was an ironmaster's house connected with the later Tudor furnace; this is now Oldlands Farm.

In 1658 a Thomas Nutt of Buxted Parish was allowed common rights on the Forest of 73 acres for his 45 cattle (a large amount), and he is believed to have owned Oldlands then; one of his descendants, R. Holford (who did not live on the estate anyway) sold it to Coventry Patmore in 1866. He ran into financial difficulties and it was bought by Alexander Nesbitt, who in 1870 built the present Oldlands Hall, and lived there some years before it became the property of a Spanish grandee—Bonaventura Paula Misa, a sherry merchant. It then passed to a South African magnate, Sir Frederick Eckstein, Bart., whose son, Sir Bernard Eckstein, added the chancel and tower of Fairwarp church in 1935–6 in memory of his father. I talked about the tower to the owner of Victoria Cottage, Dodd's Bank, a commoner on the Forest with a small farm, who worked with his father on the scaffolding. What he told me was an interesting reflection of work in rural Sussex in those pre-war days. They were paid 10d (just over 4p) an hour for the first fifty feet of height and 1/– (5p) for the remainder after that. He told me that they had great difficulty in obtaining the long timber locally, and the contracting firm from Horley had to get the long scaffold poles from Norway, the timber being still green. The contract price for the additions was £20,000, which seems considerable. Another problem was the foundations, for although on Ashdown Beds, they must have struck a clay lens which meant using steel girders.

In 1937 Sir Bernard planted an avenue of trees from the upper lodge and built the big entrance gates both at Fairwarp and Heron's Ghyll. At one time these had a cotton-flower emblem on them, a reminder of the Ecksteins' interest in Sudanese cotton growing.

Sir Bernard died in 1948, and Oldlands Hall was sold for £30,000 to a Hove buyer who converted it into flats. It would seem that the name Oldlands has had quite a confusing history for, apart from Coventry Patmore's house changing its name in 1869 from Oldlands House and Hall to Heron's Ghyll, I saw this notice on a gate off the Crowborough road in March 1982: 'Oldlands Leys NOT Oldlands Hall, Oldlands Nurseries, Oldlands Farm' . . . sic transit gloria mundi.

Duddleswell, an old name meaning Dudell's spring, was one of the six medieval walks of the old Deer Forest, and a Royal Manor; but it has always really been a collection of small farms and isolated houses. Duddleswell Manor is a nineteenth-century building, but opposite it there was once an old house, and nearby apparently lie the remains of the rather mysterious Dudeney Chapel. In 1855 some remains of an old large building were unearthed by a tenant of one of the small farms in a field, and the Reverend Edward Turner of Maresfield, an archaeologist, thought that some of the carved fragments might be ecclesiastical.

Later in the nineteenth century the greatest changes were really on the private estates, but the better roads and the extension of the railways from East Grinstead (which had first arrived there in 1855, to Ashurst in 1862, Tunbridge Wells in 1866, and from there via Crowborough to Uckfield in 1868) meant that the Forest dwellers were in better touch with the outside world, even though their open landscape had changed but little since 1693.

However, there was a certain amount of rural extractive industry such as quarrying and brickmaking on the Forest;

there were brickworks at Chuck Hatch owned by the de la Warr family whose products went down to help develop Bexhill on the coast. At Nutley in the 1860s a 25-foot seam of clay in the Ashdown Beds was dug for making bricks, near where iron ore had been dug centuries earlier. Many small quarries were extracting the massive Ashdown sandstone which was sometimes found within the beds like the one half a mile south of Marlpits and the several quarries near Jumper's Town. One worth seeing is near Gills Lap, which is picturesquely overgrown, whose stone went to build many squatters' cottages at this period for a few pounds; nowadays they fetch astonishing prices.

The rather controversial question of sheep-grazing on the open heathland seems to have been overcome by a Colonel Young from Hartfield who introduced them, and after 1900 they became 'commonable' Bernard Hale, also from Hartfield, pioneered Shetland cattle on the Forest.

Then suddenly in 1876 the uneasy peace like a dormant volcano erupted with the famous letter to the Commoners from the Lord of the Manor, now the 7th Earl de la Warr, stating that litter-cutting must cease.

Once more the fight was on, this time as an extremely long and arduous test case between his lordship and the Commoner, Mr Bernard Hale, Deputy Lieutenant of Sussex, before the High Court. The ruling was a blow to the Commoners—it laid down that litter-taking was a right only for cattle by mouth, and pointed out that the 1693 decree did not refer to any litter-cutting. So his lordship had won—but had he?

An appeal was lodged in 1881, and this time the defendants won their case by proving that it was at least a sixty-year-old custom—although a custom is not a common right. To make quite sure, the other Commoners brought a cross action against the Lord of the Manor, but this time it was a solid phalanx which included Hale again, Sir Percy Maryon-Wilson Bart. (whose family we met in Chapter 5) and Robert Melville, with support in the background from other notable Commoners like the Duke of Norfolk, the 3rd Earl of Sheffield, Lady Shelley and the 3rd Baron Colchester of Kidbrooke Park. This time Earl de la Warr came to terms and in 1885 the dispute was settled by an Act of

Parliament which regulated the Commons under the earlier Commons Act of 1876.

The important outcome was yet another landmark in the Forest's history, that is the formation of a Board of Conservators who would administer the area by levying a rate from the Commoners on an acreage basis. The Act provided for a number of things that go to make up the Forest today as we know it, the first being right of public access to many prominent landmarks on the Forest, including the famous Scots pine clumps that I have mentioned earlier. Next was the making of enclosures for cricket grounds for recreation of the main villages in the area; Fords Green at Nutley, Thompsett's Bank at Forest Row, Chelwood Gate and Fairwarp. But perhaps the most significant result was the virtual legal recognition of what had been going on for centuries, and this was the eternal nibbling practice of 'grab enclosure'.

If you look around the Forest and its margins, at places like Jumper's Town—a name that speaks for itself—you will see many cottages dotted here and there that had come into existence by this method. If a forester had a cottage on the Forest his wood stack was put close to the garden fence during the spring, and then the fence taken up in the summer and put outside and thus a piece of land was gained. Another little dodge was by fencing a haystack during the night, and claiming it as their own land, or by moving a hedge that bordered an orchard and gaining a piece of common for pasture or haymaking. Help would be needed of course to do these things quickly, but the whole family would pile in until the task was finished.

The Lord of the Manor turned a blind eye to this land grabbing, and some kind of legality was obtained by paying a small fee to him at the next Court Baron or Assembly of the freehold tenants, when the land was 'sot' or set in. If an election was in the offing, grabbing was often actively encouraged by his steward whose price for this Nelsonian act was 'voting right'.

If an actual cottage was wanted on the Forest itself, the traditional squat was quickly to build a ditch and bank enclosure, a shelter of thatched heather and to have smoke coming out of the chimney within twenty-four hours. The house was then 'finished off' with marl and local Ashdown sandstone.

One of the present Forest Ranger's cottages, belonging to Mr

R. Montague, near Barnsgate was built by this method. Incidentally he and his wife Anne-Marie are extremely competent photographers (some of the photographs in this book were taken by them) with a deep knowledge of wildlife and vegetation on the Forest. He told me the cottage was built in the traditional squatter's manner before the 1885 Act, and in fact they found an 1886 newspaper in the roof timbers.

Under the Act all who could prove that they owned land on the Forest before 9th December 1869 could keep their holdings free of any charge. Those who had illegally enclosed land since then could buy it at a fair market price. As one can imagine, there were some remarkably strange sales; one family who had enclosed seventeen separate plots paid £88, and a John Bashford of Forest Row paid £30 for a stone quarry. One Nutley resident, Albert Turner, was quite happy to buy his 1¼ acres for £88. All in all, over 150 enclosures of 33½ acres were made by 104 people.

The new Conservators certainly did not have an easy job ahead of them as many of the old depredations continued, such as purloining of wood, stone being dug and turf damaged, apart from the eternal risk of fires—often maliciously started—and continual complaints. And they seemed unable to have prevented the beginnings of the incredibly untidy growth of Crowborough which had actually spread over on to Forest land about 1904 and was even then described as 'populous and over built'.

It is surprising that on such a windy open expanse as the Forest there have not been many windmills, although they existed at one time on the fringes at East Grinstead, Ashurstwood and Selsfield Common. However, there was Nutley Mill, not recorded before 1840 when a Henry Selford worked it. This was a black post mill of early type which ground corn for the local small-holders; but its origins are mysterious, for it is thought that it came from Goudhurst in Kent, although a descendant of the family said that his grandfather had brought it from Crowborough. Both assertions could be true, for at one time it was quite common to move windmills considerable distances. Nutley Mill was only a ruin by 1908, but so very well restored from 1969 by the Nutley Preservation Society that they won a Heritage Award in 1975, and it was grinding corn again in 1972. It makes a very fine modern landmark on the Forest.

Even by 1912 the quiet and lonely Forest landscape was still much the same as it had been, because the main London road had not yet been diverted in a straight line across the heathland from Wych Cross to Nutley. The traffic went off towards Chelwood Gate, along what is now the A275, and for many years the old toll gatehouse remained in between the fork of the two roads.

Then came the 1914–18 war leaving some scars on the landscape to remind people of it, such as training trenches which were dug on Stone Hill below the Duddleswell road; south of New Pond Cottages there were rifle butts near the Crowborough road, and dugouts were made on St John's Common at Crowborough town. Evidently damage must have been caused, for later the War Office paid out £1,000 damages—a large sum over sixty years ago.

For what life in or near the Forest between the two wars, you cannot do better than read A. A. Milne's two books, *Winnie the Pooh* and *The House at Pooh Corner*, for here in disguised children's fiction is a true description of the Forest and its streams. And for the background to this then read *The Enchanted Places* by his son, Christopher Milne (1974).

The family bought the old Queen Anne Cotchford Farm in 1925; the name here means 'enclosure by the thicket'. The house had been rescued and 'done up'—the word 'restored' was not current then—by a man called Jervis. This process later went on all over the Weald. The Milnes' land reached the river we have become familiar with in this book: the tributary of the Medway with its varied names, Millbrook, Three Wards Brook and the one I favour—Steel Forge River. And here I can add a fourth, the Posingford Stream. Over this stream was a rather rickety wooden bridge built in 1907, which has come to be known as Poohsticks Bridge, and I suppose is now really part of Ashdown Forest folklore. The bridge was restored in 1979 by the generosity of the National Westminster Bank for the East Sussex County Council, and is still a very pretty spot (although not actually within the Forest itself, being north of Posingford Wood).

Christopher Milne has described how in those halcyon days of boyhood they had the Forest almost to themselves, and he remarked that Pooh would not have cared for the modern Forest with its picnic parties and transistor radios; nor would I if I were Pooh either, but that is the price of progress and another story.

At that time the region was—by our present standards—isolated, but not really for there was the very pleasant railway line from East Grinstead through Forest Row to Ashurst, a bus at Hartfield, and of course bicycles and legs. However, isolated as it was the Forest evidently still needed protection, because new bye-laws were introduced in 1935 which forbade the digging up of primroses and bluebells and removing heather, moss and rushes. The Commoners were once again reminded of past struggles about cutting litter for they were forbidden to cut bracken (called brakes) between May and June—this now seems strange to us in the light of its recent spread over the Forest—and to cut litter between May and August, except for the special areas outlined by the Conservators.

There was an interesting minor event in 1936 when a solicitor named Philip Fooks built on to an old cottage near Boringwheel Mill in Cackle Street a new house which he called Boringwheel, and he also instituted a Domestic Oratory (Catholic). Its connection with the iron industry and modern use we shall come to in the next two chapters.

The 1939–45 war brought modern warfare much closer to the Forest than its predecessor had done, for this time it was a war of the air, and there would be a constant danger of fire on the open forest. Mr Bassett, an old blacksmith and voluntary fireman of long standing whom we shall meet at Wadhurst in the next chapter, remembers being called out for an oil bomb that fell in Crowborough Warren, and many times for fires at Crowborough Beacon. Inevitably aircraft crashed on to the Forest; a Blenheim bomber came down on Broadstone Warren, and a United States Flying Fortress made a forced landing in the Convent grounds, as they were then, of Ashdown Park.

A poignant reminder of those days is the stone-walled enclosure, known as the Airman's Grave, in the middle of the open heathland between Nutley and Duddleswell, and down a track leading from the Hollies on the Duddleswell road. In the midst of a tiny garden is a white cross in memory of Sergeant Sutton, R.A.F., aged 24, of 142 Bomber Squadron and his five comrades who died when their plane crashed on the last day of

July 1941; this memorial was erected by his mother.

Later in the war a V1 flying bomb, known as a 'Doodlebug', fell at King's Standing, and brought down the ceiling at New Pond Cottages, as Mrs Seymour recalled when I talked to her about life on the Forest.

The Forest landscape was again used for training, rifle ranges being set up from the Garden of Eden to near Old Lodge; the target banks are still there, and evoke memories for some ex-Home Guard local residents who trained with the Canadians. American tanks ground over the open heathland and unfortunately caused great destruction, and another scar is the site of the old emergency airstrip which lies half a mile north-east of Chelwood Vachery, a great bare patch of eroded soil that has been gullied by heavy rainfall. Not far away is a curious relic, the remains of a light tank of 1919 vintage, which was buried so that just the gun and turret were visible, and used against aircraft. This was discovered by Alan Morriss, himself a civil airline pilot and the owner of Pippingford Park.

Even this last war changed but little the nature of the landscape or the wonderful sense of space and isolation that one got by walking over the heathland, and I can remember walking for long distances not long after the war without seeing anybody except a few cattle and sheep. In those days people reached the Forest by train, and walked up from any of the Medway valley stations like Hartfield or Withyham—an arrangement which nowadays I suppose would be considered highly inconvenient.

Changes were coming, however, which to the older Commoners and villagers of its fringes would be different from anything that had happened before in their lives, and if they did but know it in the long history of the Forest itself. In 1949 an Act provided for the restricted use of the Forest by the Army; Britain still had National Service, and the troops had to be trained somewhere. Later in the 1960s the War Office ceased using the open areas of common, but it still leased land within the private estates.

An increasing menace in the post-war years was that of heath fires, usually at their worst in spring; they were dangerous, expensive and hard work for the County Fire Brigade. In 1957 the Nature Conservancy declared that whilst strictly controlled fires at certain times might be beneficial, uncontrolled fires were 'an evil to both man and to nature'. This cut right across the centuries-old belief that fire is essential to the survival of open heath for grazing—although so it is if grazing ceases—but otherwise its benefits are few and its damage great, especially to wildlife and plants.

In 1961 the Sussex Naturalists Trust drew up a document on proposals for managing the Forest on a different basis to try and meet the needs of all concerned—somewhat optimistic within the context of modern life—and the growing threat, but then not realized, of saturation of south-eastern England. What it did do was to rouse local people to the value of their unique area that was Ashdown, and so was formed the Friends of Ashdown Forest. This association raised funds which provided the means of cutting wide fire-breaks to prevent the disappearance of rare birds and plants whose habitats were always threatened by any kind of fire. These later became fire-rides, and with the tenfold increase in fifteen years of horse riding, which at times causes considerable erosion by steel-shod hooves (not to mention that caused by walkers), these areas have become something of an emotive subject on the Forest.

Far more ominous was the colossal rise in private mobility caused by the over-use and convenience of the horse's mechanical brother—the motor car. This was distinctly aided by the ridiculous slaughter of the local branch-line railways during the disastrous Beeching-Marples era, on the grounds of economy—often completely spurious—especially as they had been given vastly improved train services in the 1950s; then a complete volte-face in railway policy caused at first downright discouragement of use, followed by complete closure.

Meantime changes were taking place on commons throughout England, and in 1965 an Act made it necessary for commons registration, where right of common existed. The Conservators of course registered the whole of Ashdown as Common Land, but individual Commoners had to register their own claims as well. The actual *number* of Commoners had risen mightily since the hundred that stood fast in 1885, owing to the breaking up of individual properties and then the building of separate houses on them giving right of common to each dweller; but fewer and fewer Commoners were using this age-old right. What seemed extraordinary was that two years after registration there were

1,300 Commoners on Ashdown, in spite of the fact that many had failed to register, thereby losing their right of common. I have often wondered what would have happened if all these people had chosen to buy cattle and sheep and use their rights of grazing. We may even have got our railways back if the roads had become choked with droving cattle and sheep—what a glorious thought! But since then the number of Commoners has dropped by half, although at 650 is still quite high.

In 1974 another Act brought the local authorities in the persons of East Sussex County Council and the new District Councils (here Wealden, based at Crowborough) on to the Board of Conservators, in return for financial support, and the number of elected Commoners was reduced to five.

Perhaps the most significant result of the rise of the motor car has been to bring the Forest into the sphere of influence of the Great Wen, to paraphrase Cobbett, and this has meant that the surrounding fringe of the Forest has been opened to the invasion of those who had the means to buy properties at inflated prices, which few people locally could afford. And this has meant, as one writer in 1971 put it, 'Ashdown Forest is rapidly becoming part of the "commuter country" whose life-roots lie in the grey streets of the City and not in the Wealden countryside.'

This is the end, for the moment, of the history of the Ashdown Commons, but there is another Ashdown history—that of the lands that have been enclosed since 1693—which is vastly different and sometimes complicated, but because of the variety and characteristics of the owners over the years is extremely interesting.

The largest award was Pippingford and Old Lodge originally purchased in the 1660s by William Newham of Maresfield but later broken into separate estates.

Since then Pippingford has had many owners and uses—including ironworking—and for a while its coppiced woods were still bordered by the old horse road that ran from East Grinstead to Rotherfield (which was used occasionally). The estate is on the infertile Ashdown sands and pebble beds, but was later bought by William Bradford who tried to improve the land as well as building a mansion on it. At his death it was sold to Henry Shirley, who added to the house, but it was destroyed by fire in 1836 before he had time to enjoy it. Its successor, the present house, was designed by a Frenchman called Hector Horeau; now much modified and slightly forlorn it still commands very fine views over the wooded landscape. A later owner, Captain Banbury, tried to establish ravens in these woods—one part is still called Ravenswood—but they died out here because their real habitat is in Ireland and the wilder Atlantic fringe of the British Isles. Earlier in this century another owner, a timber speculator called Anderson, tried to breed ospreys, but the last was seen in 1914; Ashdown is probably beyond their breeding range.

In 1918 the estate, now about 1,000 acres and forming a game reserve, was bought by Morriss, a China bullion broker, who died in 1960. He let some of the land out for soft-fruit farming—gooseberries and raspberries—which is a good use on light soils, and in recent years fruit farms have flourished at Nutley and Wych Cross. The estate mansion became a guest house, and in 1977 was leased to a commercial firm (Design and Partnership); part of the land has been leased to the Army for some years. The present owner, Alan Morriss, is enterprising, imaginative and deeply interested in wildlife, and you can find out about the modern use of the estate in the last chapter of this book.

The next largest estate, Crowborough Warren, borders the eastern fringes of the Forest; it was originally leased to Thomas Raymond in 1678. Not much more was heard about it until the eighteenth century when another 'improver' called Halls tried to use the land for arable farming but without much success. Then in the early nineteenth century an enterprising City man named Edward Trisley Howis enclosed it with plantations of conifers and deciduous trees—much its best use. He was an energetic man who used to leave London on horseback between 2 and 3 a.m., change his horse at the Godstone turnpike, and ride to Crowborough for breakfast and to see to his estate, leaving for London again in the evening. Later he lived at Hanover House, which is quite close to Crowborough Beacon, and built an elaborate five-storey water mill on the site of the former iron furnace within the Warren. This he did by enlarging the lake and building up the original bay with massive stonework, and by diverting several small watercourses to feed the millponds, so that a converging fan of little streams was cleverly and ingeniously constructed.

Howis died in 1830, but his mill (known as the New Mill) became quite famous and in 1840 had the privilege of grinding the flour for Queen Victoria's wedding cake; this was proudly told to me by Mrs Seymour of New Pond Cottages on the Forest, who had remembered the mill in its heyday. For its career continued; later it was driven by steam and, adding to its old history of casting iron and grinding corn, it became a sawmill. Some of the wood was used by local coopers in their honourable local trade of making beer barrels. The mill finally ceased working about 1948, its final demise coming when it was demolished to make 5,000 fireplaces out of the solid stonework; these are now no doubt part of the urban landscape of Crowborough.

Even after 1948 a use was found for the old furnace bay and mill dam, for on it was perched some thatched tearooms known as the Elizabethan Barn, but these were removed later to the more elegant surroundings of Tunbridge Wells. Thus the mill dominated Crowborough Warren estate's history for well over a century, and today its extensive woodlands are owned by a forestry company, with paths and bridleways amongst its pleasant verdure, and it is very hard to realize that the untidy urban sprawl of Crowborough is so close.

The estate known today as Broadstone Farm started life as Broadstone Walk, one of the great medieval walks of the old Deer Park, before being combined with Pippingford in 1693. By 1747 it had become Broadstone Ground, and later Broadstone Lodge when it was bought by Lord de la Warr in 1778.

However, by far its most interesting owner was Walter Johnson, who bought it from the de la Warrs in 1906; by this time it was about 150 acres in extent. In 1909 he built a large 'Victorian'-type house which he called Broadstone Place, but this was pulled down in 1946.

Johnson was a clever electrical engineer and one of the founders of the famous firm of Johnson & Phillips of Charlton, then in Kent, now London. He was an extremely colourful character—larger than life—an early pioneer in the use of electrical power and his life was so full of incidents that they would fill a very large book. Broadstone Place was his country estate after he had become a prosperous businessman (for he had started from quite small beginnings). He built two narrow-gauge electric railways for the estate, one of which was known as the G.W.R.; on its opening day there was a typical Johnsonian incident. The loco he was driving got out of control and hit a tree. He jumped clear, but it was a shock for a young man from the estate who was courting his girlfriend behind it—he is still alive today and remembers the event well.

Once when Johnson was a much younger man living near the works at Charlton, and travelling from there to New Cross Station by hansom or trap, he got bored with waiting at the station, and jumped on a train passing slowly through. He landed on the lap of the Empress of France. The Emperor was not amused (though she may have been). After chatting with them the train arrived at Charing Cross and Johnson, seeing the red carpet, promptly jumped out and escaped into the crowd. Many years later, about 1910, he acquired a special Daimler car, originally built for the Sultan of Zanzibar who had died before he could use it. It was white with a drawing room saloon, movable armchairs and a panelled roof; naturally it always attracted immediate and enormous attention. Once whilst it stood at the roadside unattended in Uckfield surrounded by the usual crowd of gapers a charming young lady, well known socially, could not resist putting her head through the window to have a look. Johnson arrived, took her by the elbow and escorted her inside to ask her opinion. She was extremely embarrassed—but remember this was 1910! One further eccentric occasion was when he had to chair a Board meeting and overslept at his club; so he arrived without his tie—very *infra dig.* in those days—and promptly made one out of blotting paper, which he dotted with ink.

Today the farm is still an interesting place. A cannon ball was found there from the pioneer Newbridge furnace, and there is a chestnut tree in which is embedded a huge old Admiralty pattern anchor that Johnson brought back from the Indian Ocean, dredged up by a cable ship in which he was serving.

A rather different type of estate of no great age is Ashdown Park. This has had an extraordinary variety of owners. It was first owned in 1830 by a Captain Henniker, and in 1867 a huge, Gothic, massive and romantic house was built there. Some have called it gloomy, but I think it fits its surroundings rather well. In the nearby woods there was an estate church (dedicated to Sir Richard de Wyck) built in the Perpendicular style, but it became ruined and is now demolished. The estate once appeared in Bradshaw as 'Forest Row for Ashdown Park and Forest 3 miles'. Afterwards an order of nuns, the Sisters of Notre Dame de Namur, were there for about forty years and became very popular. They built their own convent church and a school for local Forest children, but financial reasons forced them to leave in 1967. Then it became an American University; and now it is a training centre for Barclays Bank, who maintain its grounds in immaculate condition. I met a most cheerful Durham coal-miner's son who is a gardener there after having spent many years in France attending the war graves in many cemeteries; he was very content with his outdoor life.

One of the smaller enclosures was the 33-acre area that became Kidbrooke Park. This had been a small clearing for the herding of young deer from the Forest. Its main interest for us is how a wild landscape was changed into a highly ornamental artificial designed late-eighteenth-century estate, which very cleverly recreated the romantic side of the natural scene. It was begun by a house built in 1724 by Robert Mylne, the architect of Blackfriars Bridge, for William Nevill of East Grinstead. He had unexpectedly become Lord Abergavenny through the death of a cousin, and because the family estate at Eridge was very rundown he moved to Kidbrooke Park. Mylne altered the house, and later Humphrey Repton laid out a large park from land bought close to Hindleap Warren, but one effect of the famous 1693 decree was apparent, for common land lying in between prevented the full extent of the plans from being carried out. However, Repton designed a splendid water and tree landscape with gardens, lakes, cascades and many groups of hardwoods, conifers and exotics were planted. By 1790 Eridge was restored and the Nevills moved back there. Kidbrooke Park then decayed and at length in 1805 was bought by Charles Abbott, later Lord Colchester and the Speaker of the House of Commons. In 1874 Henry Freshfield bought it from the Abbotts and he later became the first Chairman of the Board of Conservators of Ashdown Forest. His son Douglas, a keen mountaineer, laid out a 'wild garden' using original trees from the Forest and planting Tulip and Sweet Gum (Liquid Amber).

In 1909 it was bought by L. P. Kerewich who lost his three sons during the war that followed, and the house became a base camp on the Forest.

Then in 1921 the Norwegian banker Olaf Hambro acquired the estate, and during the next seventeen years this became the great 'swan song' of Kidbrooke Park when all kinds of gardens were laid out and developed like paved, walled, tropical, bog and water varieties by the Hambros who were very keen gardeners. They were helped by materials and labour being easily obtained—not to mention the favourable climate of the period.

During this time in England there was great interest in historical pageants, which were acted in places with a long historical pedigree like Greenwich, where one was held at night—a sort of forerunner of the 'Son et Lumière' festivals which fit the great houses and châteaux of Britain and France so well. In July 1929 Kidbrooke Park was chosen by Lord Edward Gleichen to present 'Ashdown Forest through the Ages' in nine episodes. Vita Sackville-West wrote the prologue spoken by the 'Spirit of Anderida', and then followed Ancient Britons, Henry VIII and galloping Excise men with the final episode being played by Christopher Milne, then aged nine, walking down through the trees into the arena carrying the toys his father's books had made so famous. There was a distinguished audience which included the present Queen Mother and Rudyard Kipling, and the old Southern Railway ran special trains and cheap fares to the now defunct Forest Row station.

In 1938 the house ceased to have private owners and passed to an insurance company, and at length became the Michael Hall Rudolph Steiner School, which sold off some of the estate land for private building on the edge of the Forest. There are still vestiges left of the once grand park-like gardens which well reflect a period in the Forest's history when courtly mansions have been set amid the wilder Forest and the setting gradually changed to one of sophisticated gardening splendour; there is no place for this in today's society.

There are many other properties around the Forest with houses that represent all styles of architecture, some interesting, some pretentious and some recent (one or two of which raise queries of how planning permission was obtained—not to build, but why such unsuitable styles in the Forest environment were ever allowed).

Wych Cross Place, built by Douglas Freshfield round about 1900, had some fine gardens laid out from advice by the famous Gertrude Jekyll who worked at Nymans, Handcross.

Right over on the western side of the Hindleap Road is a rather good example of a house—of no great age—but built in a pleasing Sussex vernacular style. This is Cripps Manor, a gabled stone building, with a tiled roof and hung mechanicals with outlying stables set in a wide tree-fringed open space against the background of Horncastle Wood, inside which people once dug for iron ore. Cripps Manor was up for sale when I last saw it, and it would be nice to think that its future use would fit the Forest, rather than the Forest being made to fit an alien use.

Further east and off the main A22 is Chelwood Vachery, once associated with Micheleham Priory. The house is old—fifteenth century—but not as old as the Vachery whose name is old French for a dairy farm and a reminder of an early Norman penetration into the Forest.

Finally, not only is there a variety of houses, but an equal variety of owners, who for different reasons desire the Forest as a setting for their activities. Here are two examples, one connected with the mind and the other with the body. At Greenwood Gate, near the Clump of the same name, off the B2188 and amid the trees in a secluded spot is the headquarters of a modern version of a seventeenth-century order of philosophers of German origin—the Rosicrucians. On the road to Friar's Gate at Crowborough St John's is the Horder Centre, founded by Miss Bocherek in 1954. This had its first patients' centre in 1966 at Windlesham Manor, Conan Doyle's old home. Now they are on the Forest in a pleasant, if rather plain, building where I talked to the Administrator, Miss Beaumont, who explained that it was entirely a charity and few patients pay the full cost. They have beds for thirty-nine here, and rehabilitation is provided at Eastbourne General Hospital. It is named after their first president, Lord Horder, Britain's most famous rheumatologist. I must admit to having a special interest, as I was a sufferer from this all too common and often disregarded illness.

And here I end this survey of the history of Ashdown Forest, a region that the famous historian William Camden evidently knew but little for in his *Britannia* written between 1586 and 1607 he declares: 'Having thus surveyed the coast of Sussex, nothing remains to be mentioned in the inland parts but extensive woods and forests, the remains of the antient Sylva Anderida.'

9

Ironworking on the Forest and in Sussex—Prehistoric to Present

Iron has been mined, smelted, forged and cast in the Weald for 2,500 years, and at one time our area of Sussex was the most important iron producer in Britain.

In spite of its long history it was always a rather sporadic industry which reached peaks in Roman and Tudor times. The record is scanty during the Saxon period and again in medieval times when it must have been dramatically affected by the two outbreaks of the Black Death. Nevertheless, traces are beginning to be revealed by some exciting modern archaeological discoveries on both Ashdown Forest and the surrounding Wealden countryside.

The basic raw material was of course ironstone, the richest deposits being siderite and found in the lower part of the Wadhurst Clay. This particular rock of clays and soft shales is something of a geological layer cake with its beds of silt, sandstone and even some limestone. An example of limestone is tufa round a spring in Stumletts Pit Wood, north of Huggets Furnace.

It is spread out over the High Weald roughly in the shape of a horseshoe, its broken outcrops beginning westwards at East Grinstead and Horsted Keynes and extending eastwards in two arms, one through Wadhurst to Rye, and the other further south through Uckfield to Hastings.

This Wadhurst Clay country is often the typical green and

pleasant Wealden valley landscape, but its looks belie its fertility for the soils are heavy and ill-drained, so the fields are often pasture.

It was the chief source of Wealden iron, but not the only one for ore was worked from the iron pan in the Ashdown sands and later from the stiff and heavy Weald Clay.

For 2,000 years rough wrought iron was made by a primitive process which hardly changed from Iron Age Celts through to medieval Englishmen. It consisted, briefly, of the ore being mixed with charcoal on a round hearth, and covered with clay. The smelting was helped by bellows, which produced a spongy mass or bloom (Old English *bloma*, a bloom). This was removed from the slag and hammered into shape; the bloomery slag was often so rich in iron that in later times it could be smelted again. The word 'slag', it seems, came from an old German word *slagge* connected with hammering or striking. The bloomery process continued down the ages into Tudor times and even lingered on into the seventeenth century. But herein lies a mystery, for water power in the late Middle Ages had been applied to some of these bloomeries in parts of England like Northumberland, but so far no real evidence has been found of such water-powered bloomeries in the Weald. That is, unless the recently discovered forge at Woolbridge, near Mayfield, with a bay in the infant Rother valley, turns out to be one, for typical bloomery slag has been found there, but nothing else.

However, it was a revolutionary process that succeeded the bloomery, and it came to England in the late fifteenth century from France, originating in Lorraine, or perhaps even earlier in Liège, now eastern Belgium. This great landmark in the iron industry was the blast furnace driven by water power which produced cast iron by crushing the ore, working the bellows and hammer. The cast iron was then poured forth into sand moulds and a casting pit. If wrought iron was needed, the molten metal was cast into large triangular sectioned castings called 'sows', the smaller castings being known as 'pigs'. These were then forged by a water-powered hammer.

The very first furnace of this type was set up by the initiative of the first Tudor King, Henry VII. It was to prepare for his Scottish campaign and was sited at Newbridge in Hartfield parish inside Ashdown Forest on the Millbrook or Steel Forge river that flows into the Medway. The furnace was in blast by 1496, and worked by skilled French ironfounders, but history is rather vague as to what was actually cast there, although most certainly cannon balls were made to replace the earlier 'gun-stones'—actually made of stone.

These missiles fired from rather primitive guns made from wrought-iron strips had failed miserably against the superior French cannon cast by a process then unknown in England. Earlier in the century Henry VII's Plantagenet ancestor, Henry VI (1422–61), had seen his armies literally blasted out of his French possessions by this same artillery in 1449–50. The French cannon were directed by the brothers Jean and Gaspard Bureau, the great master Gunners of Charles VII, who destroyed sixty castles in four days.

Whilst this chapter was being written the Tudor warship *Mary Rose* was being raised from the Solent amid all the glare of modern publicity, and it is a very real possibility that the cannon balls found in her were cast at Newbridge on Ashdown or nearby at one of the Hartfield furnaces like Parrock.

The new process at once shifted the geographical position of the sites from where iron and clay could be found to suitable water-power sites, which led to the Weald becoming the centre of ironmaking for a long time in Britain. The bellows of the blast furnace and the hammer for the forge were operated by water wheels needing a good flow of water, and this was done by using the deep little incised valleys or ghylls of the Weald. These are very common in the sandstone country of the High Weald, as in Ashdown Forest and the surrounding slopes and ridges. Being narrow and steep the streams often rush down to the valley floor in a series of steps that could be dammed by bays to form ponds—either for the bellows or the hammer or both, sometimes near each other on the same stream.

Thus the Weald for some centuries—in spite of the changing fortunes of war and peace—became a scattered, but important industrial area, for north of London the vast deposits of lean iron ore lay untouched beneath the Jurassic scarplands of the Midlands, their slopes being grazed by millions of sheep. Beyond here the ores deep within the Staffordshire and South Wales coalfields were hardly worked until the pioneer industrialist Abraham Darby in Shropshire discovered the art of smelting with coke instead of charcoal in 1730. And as he was a devout Quaker he kept his discovery quiet for some years, having a great fear of it being used to forge weapons. And outside the Weald the only really rich ores Britain had, such as the haematite of Furness and the Lake District, were not used until the rise of steel ships in the nineteenth century.

The later decline of the Wealden ironmaking—though like Charles II it was 'an unconscionable time a-dying'—was due, like so many things in history, to a combination of events rather than any particular single reason. Some historians and many school textbooks of course are always searching for a nice tidy generalized reason or a really suitable dramatic event to explain things. The vision of grimy Sussex ironworkers cutting down vast quantities of greenwood for fuel has always persisted as a popular image in Wealden history—however inaccurate it may have been.

The last furnace in Sussex, that of Ashburnham, survived until 1827, but earlier in 1761 the famous Carron ironworks had begun in Scotland casting cannon from coke-fired furnaces, and taking skilled men from Sussex. But at first they had many failures, and it was not until they produced the famous Carronade about 1779 that they superseded the Wealden gunfounders who could not compete, in spite of the strenuous efforts of the ironmaster Dr Rose Fuller, of the famous Heathfield family of gunfounders, who was confident that the gun trade would be restored to Sussex.

Ironworking, however, did not cease within the Weald, it merely became a local enterprise instead of an industrial one and got its iron from outside, although there were two attempts to revive the industry. The first, in 1857, was by mining ore from the Ashdown Beds at Snape Wood near Wadhurst, conveniently close to a railway cutting, and then sending it to Staffordshire to be smelted. The enterprise lasted just a year, being abandoned in September 1858, but as we saw in Chapter 5 it led to some interesting memories.

The second attempt was in 1908, and never got beyond the survey stage for the Earl of Sheffield hoped to revive ironworking on his estate at Sheffield Park, and commissioned a Professor Gregory to investigate the prospects of both mining and smelting. The Professor rejected the idea on sheer economic grounds as he thought the vein far too thin to be worked. For which, I suppose, many people must be very grateful, as the beauty of the later Sheffield Park Gardens is probably far more profitable, and at the very least more aesthetically pleasing, than the prospects of making the place rather grubby like its larger namesake in Yorkshire.

Two events in the eighteenth century made the local blacksmith in Sussex an indispensable member of the community. One was the agricultural revolution which had followed the vast increase in the enclosure movement. This had brought improvements needing many more iron implements—horse hoes, drills and rakes, ploughs and harrows. And even if he did not make them, the blacksmith was often called upon to mend them.

The other event was the coming of the Turnpike Trusts with metalled roads which ushered in the jolly and rather expensive era of coaching with the many horses that needed shoeing. So the Sussex blacksmiths were kept busy thus until the early 1930s, and although the motor age naturally brought a decline the trade has never quite died out.

Today in the 1980s there is a great increase and interest in horse ownership—particularly in our part of the county—with of course the need for shoeing, but much of this is done now on a travelling basis. So the blacksmiths are still in business, though perhaps really it is a leisure or luxury trade.

We must now return to the ancient bloomeries in our area, which go back over 2,000 years, appropriately enough to the Iron Age, when the Celtic people of that era first appeared, keenly seeking iron ore.

On Ashdown Forest it seems they built a fortified camp at Garden Hill, did some iron forging, and perhaps had small furnaces for roasting the ore. Until recently very few pre-Roman bloomeries had been discovered or accurately dated, for it is difficult to distinguish between prehistoric and medieval slag—there is a time range of 1,500 years. Their dates are mainly found by pottery sherds, and I must admit as a mere geographer I have often wondered why ancient man spent so much time breaking up his pots.

Most of the prehistoric Sussex bloomeries are in the Battle-Sedlescombe area, and so are outside the region covered by this book, but there were some in the Northern Weald. These were defended sites serving a small local market, and are not far from Ashdown. For example, there is a site at Sandyden Ghyll in the woods north of Mark Cross. Let me say at once that I failed to find it! I looked for it on a hot summer's day, probably the worst time to find anything historic in the countryside because of the growth of the vegetation.

There is another much closer in Minepit Wood, near Orznash Farm north of Crowborough. This is a site that was worked intermittently over a very long period of time by Iron Age people, then early Romans and finally in the Middle Ages; it is also very difficult to find, being in a private wood.

Perhaps the most interesting site for us, which combines a pleasant walk (although a bit of a climb) is the old fort on Saxonbury Hill (662 feet), south of Frant and opposite the National Trust's Nap Wood with the A267 in between. This was a mining camp; the ore was found nearby from the Wadhurst Clay revealed by faulting against the Tunbridge Wells Sands. Saxonbury was one of a long line of Iron Age forts strung out across south-eastern England with others northwards at Castle Hill, Tonbridge and Oldbury near Ightham in Kent, whilst westwards were Dry Hill, Hascombe near Godalming and Holmbury Hill, all in Surrey. There seems to be a definite connection between them and local ironworking.

We now approach the Roman era, and the whole subject expands enormously for in recent years archaeological research and intensive field-work have revealed that the Roman iron-working was a large and important industry, and it would seem that the Romans developed the Weald probably not only for charcoal fuel but also for growing food to supply the sites. The number of bloomeries now identified and dated runs into hundreds, with many in our area, including some on the Forest itself with very recent excavations.

The first Roman ironworking site in Sussex—and also on Ashdown—was discovered in 1844 by the Reverend Edward Turner, Rector of Maresfield, and as so often happens—by accident. He came upon some workmen excavating a bed of cinders at Oldlands Farm within his parish, which were to be used on the county roads.

These finds were later described in a classic paper in 1849 by the Sussex historian and archaeologist Mark Anthony Lower. The Roman remains were many and of extraordinary variety; amongst them were coins covering a long period—AD 54 to 286—and of four Emperors: Nero, Vespasian, Tetricus and Diocletian. Some of the vast amounts of slag found there were thought to have paved the Roman road that runs across the Forest. The real significance of this large 7-acre site was not fully understood until recently, for Oldlands was almost certainly an administrative centre as well.

And this leads us to the other large site on the Forest, that of Garden Hill, which must be among the most interesting and important discoveries of recent years in Sussex.

Ironworking itself was not on such a large scale here, it seems, partly perhaps because the local Ashdown sandstone ore (iron pan) is rather sporadic, and also the needs of the inhabitants were largely domestic—for example, pots and pans.

What the excavations here did show was that the settlement must have been a fairly important administrative headquarters connected with the iron industry on Ashdown Forest and beyond. The finds range over several periods and include much varied pottery from Bronze and Iron Ages, local Romano-British and Samian and Spanish amphorae. Among the many interesting things like querns and a silver ring was an engraving in hard glass paste of the corn goddess Ceres—always an important ritual figure in Roman life. The building remains included a large wooden one that certainly ranked as a villa, and a 30-foot long stone bath-building with a tiled roof. In this was a bath with a long stoke hole, hot room, tepid room, cold room and plunge. In the hot room among the tiles were eighteen interesting baked clay spacers, one actually threaded on its iron hold-fast or support. Near the cold plunge was an almost complete Roman window pane—this very important discovery now rests in the British Museum.

Although this bath complex has been called 'rough' and is thought to be a local copy of a more elegant Roman original, one cannot help thinking it must have seemed the height of luxury to the local British Celts, and indeed if it had remained intact in the many centuries to come it would still have surprised people of the nineteenth century or even later.

In 1980 a Roman villa and ironworking complex very similar

to Garden Hill was discovered in the Viroin valley at Treignes in southern Belgium—completely by chance when a field was ploughed for the first time for several years. Its position seems to have been governed by three things: a favourable aspect, relative proximity of iron ore deposits, and near the routeway of the River Meuse. Truly, the Romans' organization was a European one!

Besides these two large sites of Oldlands and Garden Hill there have been smaller actual bloomeries discovered on the Forest in recent years, mainly on or near the large Pippingford estate. In 1972 a smelting furnace and smithy hearth were excavated at Pippingford, and the date of the pottery found showed it to be a pioneer site working for a while after the Conquest. Two others at Pippingford East Wood and Strick-edrige Gill were both on streams and perhaps the most inter-esting of all was at Cow Park on open heathland, but enclosed since 1696. This was on the side of the Steel Forge valley, after the river passes through the chain of artificial lakes in Pippingford Park that are like a string of beads. Here the indefatigable Mr Tebbutt discovered three furnaces, and the unique find in Britain of where a flat-topped anvil had been used. Today this is a very windswept and bleak place, as the excavators found, but as the probable date is first or second century the weather may have been kinder then, or the ironworkers tougher!

Beyond the Forest north of the River Medway is a large outcrop of Wadhurst Clay which led to widespread ironworking both in Roman and Tudor times. At great Cansiron Farm, close to the Cansiron stream which later runs into the Medway at Hartfield, is what appears to us to be a large field in rather a pretty rural area. It was in fact a 4-acre Roman 'industrial' site, which produced enough iron slag to metal a good deal of the London-Lewes Roman road which is to be found not far away to the east.

This little region is proving very fruitful for Roman dis-coveries, for in the summer of 1982 on Little Cansiron Farm near Holtye a Roman tile kiln was found just below the surface of a field. Through the kindness of Mr Peter Latham of Little Cansiron I was shown it, and rewarded with a nice red tile that could sit on any respectable house today without shame. Some years earlier, in 1975, the sharp eyes of his daughter Claire had discovered a cannon ball in the Cansiron stream—a relic of the Tudor furnace just beyond the bridge over the stream.

Amongst the many hundreds of sites now known, two earlier ones, originally discovered by Ernest Straker, on the fringes of Ashdown now appear to be highly significant in piecing together the story of Roman Britain. The first just north of Buxted at Morphews by the railway line produced in 1973 a hypocaust tile from a nearby stream; this single clue could mean yet another large centre like Oldlands or Garden Hill.

The second is on the banks of the Upper Medway at Ridge Hill, discovered in 1927 and considered then important enough to be railed off. Here I can modestly add that I have seen it, which it seems many archaeologists have not been able to do. The railed-off section is now rather ruined and forlorn, but I found a large lump of bloomery slag in the Medway.

Like Great Cansiron, this site was near a road, the Roman London-Brighton link which ran to the South Downs, where much corn was grown and where there were many villas. The northern end was an outlet to London for the iron market.

It is now thought that the population of Britain in the second century AD was about four million, a figure not reached again for over 1,200 years. So if we consider these really quite dramatic recent discoveries of ironworking and tile manufacture plus the road network and the strongly held view that many more villas are yet to be found in Kent, historians can no longer talk about a mere Roman occupation. We must begin surely to think that Roman Britannia was a rather more organized state than was once thought. It means, too, that progress is not automatically continuous, as in our own times technology does not seem to be going hand in hand with culture or indeed civilized living.

There is now enough evidence to consider the organization of the great Roman iron industry, which archaeologists think was in two regional groups—eastern and western Weald.

The eastern group was largely coastal and formed a large state export industry using former ports like Bodiam, and later under the control of the Roman Fleet (Classis Britannica). This is in itself a fascinating story, but does not really concern our part of Sussex.

Our area lies with the western group of Wealden sites, which

Iron graveslabs, Wadhurst Church

Mr. Bassett, Blacksmith, Durgates Forge, Wadhurst, 1982

Nightjar chick, Ashdown Forest

Marsh Gentian, Ashdown Forest

Lizard, Ashdown Forest

Adder, Pippingford Park

Dragonfly, Ashdown Forest

Highland Cow, Duddleswell

Sheep, Misbourne Farm, Ashdown Forest

Riding in the Garden of Eden

Sheep dogs, King's Standing,
Ashdown Forest

Firefighting in the Forest

Gravetye Manor

Bluebell Railway: train near Freshfield

were thought to be under civilian control and worked by licensed private enterprise. Here the iron ore was found in two ways; firstly by rivers originally cutting down their valleys and exposing it at the junction of the Wadhurst Clay and Ashdown Beds. The other was by discovery when they were building their roads, which may explain the many miles of slag paving.

After all this intense Roman activity the historical record is bare regarding Saxon ironworking in Sussex, but in 1980 a rare Middle Saxon bowl furnace from the early ninth century and two hearths were found on a stretch of open heathland in the Millbrook valley on Ashdown Forest, while water pipes were being laid.

The Domesday record for Sussex ironworking is equally bleak, for only one site is recorded in the county. This was the 'una ferraria' in the hundred of Grenested (East Grinstead) which Straker thought was the Roman bloomery of Walesbeech, now under the water of Weir Wood Reservoir.

Medieval bloomeries seem to be very little different from their prehistoric ancestors, and are usually dated by their pottery for although the ironworkers probably did not live on the sites they had to spend long hours there.

There are none on the Forest itself, for it is very unlikely that ironworking would have been allowed in a Royal hunting forest. However, there are five on the Forest fringes, three in the Crowborough area at Boarshead, Orznash and south of Crowborough Common, and two near Buxted at the High Hurstwood road and south of the station on a stream.

We have now reached the end of the bloomery period, and the question arises of the interested reader visiting them. It is a source of much vexation that these sites are NOT marked on Ordnance Survey maps nor are they recorded on the ground in any way. The recent short-sighted economy 'cuts' may account for this, and I have been told that the Department of the Environment 'know where they are', although frankly this is of little use in trying to find the sites.

There are a number of pitfalls; many are now on private land which means you must get some kind of permission if you want to indulge in 'poking about' on the site. You can of course try careful and judicious trespassing, for the countryside beyond the overcrowded roads is often empty these days with all the mechanized farming that Britain is so expensively competent with. But be warned, innocent amateurs do not appear to farmers or landowners to be any different from far less well-intentioned invaders of their property. Boots need to be stout as well as hearts and clothing rough, for the sites are often surrounded by that scourge of the landscape—barbed wire. Lastly, you will need some little knowledge and quite a vivid imagination, but there is something indefinably exciting about finding slag on a site where ancient man worked.

My own bloomery experiences are rather limited, but I will recount them for what they are worth. On Ashdown Forest itself most of the sites seem to be on private land, but a very recently discovered one is near the pond west of Camp Hill clump on open heathland. A small valley leads out of this pond, which is man-made and water has eroded the site, about 200 yards south-westwards. I did not find any slag, but while poking about in wellingtons I was overtaken by a heavy rainstorm with thunder. However, I was rewarded by superb views of the distant Downs when the storm had passed, and my impression is that there must be many sites to be discovered on the Forest—probably in remote places.

The most successful visit was to Pounsley Roman bloomery near Framfield, which I had been told was 'along the banks of a small stream'. That I found it was due to my wife, always a careful person, noticing some slag and scoria by a farm gate, which we then traced to the stream banks and found a great deal, some of which is now proudly exhibited. There is quite a feeling of exhilaration in locating the site by map in the place where it ought to be. Bloomery slag has a high iron content due to imperfect smelting; some is dull and metallic whilst other pieces are quite glossy and picturesque.

One visit which was both interesting and curious was to the large site at Great Cansiron. The farm manager was reluctant, naturally, to allow me to walk on a field with a growing corn crop—in this case oats, but I promised to be careful. However, he really need not have worried unduly, for the field had great bare patches with large lumps of slag here and there almost like rocks on a Highland croft. I found a medieval pottery fragment, and a large Roman bath tile plus enough slag to pave a private road of my own, so I was completely satisfied.

If after this you still would like to see the bloomeries in the area covered by this book, there is a list of map references in the Appendix. You will need the appropriate 2½ inch or 1:25,000 map, as anything on a smaller scale is like looking for a nail in a field.

As we saw earlier in the chapter, the water-powered blast furnace was pioneered on Ashdown Forest in early Tudor times, although its history is rather hazy, and before its operation two rather shadowy figures had appeared on the scene.

In 1493 an ironfounder, probably French for his name was Pieter Roberdes alias Graunt Pierre, had an iron mill in Hart-field—and it is just possible that this was a water-powered bloomery, for there is mention of a 'great hammer'. He became a partner of one Harry Mayer, alias Harry Fyner, a goldsmith of Southwark who it seems later set up the new furnace at New-bridge. Meanwhile Fyner had Roberdes arrested for debt, fettered in irons and confiscated most of his property, but it is more than likely that Fyner learnt his trade from the unfor-tunate Roberdes.

However, by 1496 this furnace was working on six acres of land with a watercourse, and living in tile-clad weather-boarded cottages was a little colony of French ironworkers. There was also a corn mill working at the same time, which continued long after the furnace ceased (in fact into the twen-tieth century), and at length became a private residence. The ironworkers became squatters, their cottages developed into permanent hamlets which was a pattern to be repeated in and along the fringes of Ashdown Forest and other forested areas like St Leonard's.

The banks of the dam or bay at Newbridge—which is rather a curious circular shape—can still be seen at the bottom of Kidds Hill, just before the Newbridge Splash. They were cut through by the side road from Gills Lap to Coleman's Hatch, and slag is still to be found in the vicinity.

Further upstream in Pippingford Park was the Steel Forge furnace built in 1519, also with a rather vague history, but part of a later dam is still there on the same site. This survived until 1946, but was breached by the Army trying to fish by explosives. Neither of these furnaces seemed to have worked beyond 1600, but Newbridge was mentioned in Forest Proceedings 1539 (under Henry VIII) thus:

> The iron mills called Newebridge in the Nether end of the Forest of
> Ashdown . . . that to melt the sowes in the forges of fineries there
> must be two persons . . . whereof one holdeth the work at the hammer
> and the second keepeth the work hot.

It continued: 'One man cannot keep the hammer because the
work must be kept in such hot that may not shift hands.'

All of which meant early Tudor ironworking must have been
a hot, hard and heavy business so it is not surprising that a
custom of an ale and later beer allowance became necessary.
This practice continued down the centuries into modern steel
making with the steel puddlers at Middlesbrough becoming
equally hot and thirsty, so that the town gained the reputation
of brewing the strongest beer in England, as Dortmund in the
Ruhr does likewise in Germany. What, one wonders, do the
modern computer-operated steelworkers drink now?

The next important site on the Forest was at Crowborough
Warren, where a furnace was built in the later sixteenth
century. The very high bay is still there, but the large pond just
has a trickle through it, although the site had a later eventful
history as we saw earlier in Chapter 8 when it was a watermill.
It was fairly remote until the rise of Crowborough town, but is
on a public footpath; like many of the Forest furnaces, its life
was fairly short as the Parliamentary Survey of 1657 refers to it
as the 'old Furnace'. It has an associated forge downstream at
the bottom of Marden's Hill near Friar's Gate by the road; the
bay is still there as well, and the stream heavily iron-stained,
but the pond is dry.

Way down at the southern end of the Forest on a headwater of
the River Ouse, and along Old Forge Lane off the A22, is Old
Forge and its associated furnace. This was known at one time (in
the 1574 list) as Marshalls; and it is connected with Ralph
Hogge of Buxted who owned the manor house of Marshalls
nearby. Along with Parson William Levett of Buxted, he was
the first successful ironmaster to cast cannon in England. They
both dug ore on the Forest from a seam of clay within the
Ashdown beds just south of what is now the Nutley-Duddleswell
road. The forge of this site seems to have had a long life, and was
well remembered by old people in the late nineteenth century,

but it had probably by then become a smithy. Today the 10-acre pond is a field with a riot of freshwater plants growing in it, but there is still much slag. The owner of Forge Cottage, Mr Skelton, a retired chartered accountant, very kindly and with great interest showed me the field and the man-made leat or sidestream which still exists as well as a large grassy hump in his very picturesque rose garden which was part of the old bay.

Further up the stream and down Cackle Street is a very large and beautiful lake known as Boringwheel Mill from a defunct flour mill. The name plus local tradition suggests that cannon may well have been bored there until about the 1770s. They were cast hollow and then reamed out with a special tool. One of these, 11 feet long and weighing 190 pounds, was found at Stream Mill, Chiddingly, some years ago buried in charcoal-soaked soil—it is now in the Anne of Cleves Museum at Lewes, and appears an incredible tool. Nothing like that was found at Boringwheel, but a report in the *Sussex Weekly Advertiser* of Monday, 21st November 1774 states: 'A poor man had the misfortune to have his hand shattered in a terrible manner, on Thursday morning, by the discharge of a cannon at Maresfield.'

Boringwheel is, or was, of course in the parish of Maresfield. As we saw earlier, there were several forges and furnaces in Maresfield parish besides Boringwheel and Old Forge—for example, Lower Marshalls, and the one that came to be known as Maresfield Powder Mills. This latter was casting guns for the Merchant Service in 1620, and in 1627 Monsieur Donevide, a Frenchman employed by Cardinal Richelieu, went to Maresfield to see the making and boring of guns (Boringwheel?), and tried to persuade a gunfounder to go to France—the reverse of 130 years earlier!

By the time of the Civil War ironworking seems to have completely declined on Ashdown, for no places are mentioned in the Parliamentary List of 1653. But a recent discovery shows that it must have revived again following the famous award of 1693. For in 1970 Mr Tebbutt found the remains of two furnaces in Pippingford Park on the site of the original Steel Forge furnace and later in 1974 excavated them. The results have turned out to be a most interesting piece of later history of the Forest's ironworking. Pippingford by this time—1696—had become enclosed land beyond the boundary of the present more open public commons. The earlier or western furnace was a solid square stone structure, most of it being good ashlar stone construction 26 feet square and about 5 feet high. There was an oak-lined gun-casting pit, and a stone one for the water wheel. This showed some signs of alteration, as the dam had been probably raised to give a much bigger pond and a more powerful flow.

The other furnace, the eastern one, had only its foundations left, but a complete cannon was found. This was of the two-pound or falcon type, but it was faulty with flaws on the muzzle exactly as cast. A little further away were the remains of a boring mill for reaming the cannon.

It is a mystery when exactly these furnaces were blowing and who were the gunfounders, but a lease of 1717 shows a Charles Hooper of Covent Garden letting for thirty-one years a furnace pond, house and some woodland to a Charles Manning, brass-founder of Dartford, Kent. Furthermore, CM is engraved on the cannon's trunnion, or pins by which the gun was pivoted on its carriage. This seems to be further evidence of the shifting and complicated ownership of private Forest land after 1693, and characteristic of much of Sussex today.

Let us now leave the Forest and examine the water-powered furnaces and forges in the nearby High Weald.

After the dissolution of the monasteries in 1538 there were very great changes in the ownership of property within the Weald. This led to new owners setting up ironworks, and also great Sussex landowners like the Gages and Pelhams leasing property and investing in mining rights and coppiced woods for charcoal, all of which was good sound business.

As a result there was an enormous burst of ironmaking and gunfounding to supply the ready markets wherever they happened to be: here or overseas, legal or illegal. There were also some extraordinary lawsuits regarding ironworks in the sixteenth and seventeenth centuries tried at Common Law, Chancery Court, or even in the Star Chamber if the plaintiff could include some threat, real or imaginary, to the law and order of the Crown or monarch in person.

In Tudor times, however, it was inevitable that the iron-masters would become mixed up with politics and religion, and some had their property seized by the Crown. Such was the

Admiral Lord Seymour in 1549, Master of Ordnance, and a supremely ambitious man who was Henry VIII's brother-in-law (and he had successfully married Henry's widow Catherine Parr after unsuccessful attempts to marry Elizabeth, Mary Tudor and Anne of Cleves!). He lost his ironworks at Sheffield Park, amongst others, and his head as well in Edward VI's reign (1537–53).

This forge on the Ouse (along with the furnace at Sheffield Mill) was very early, being worked largely by Frenchmen, and there is some mystery about the source of iron ore, the nearest being at Danehill; but some was brought from Chailey Common. It is probably an example of a site chosen for its water-power possibilities rather than location of iron deposits.

All this ironmaking activity caused a great complaint to be made in 1548 by the portsmen of Hastings, Rye and Winchelsea against the ironmasters. Earlier Henry VIII had set up cannon foundries in Picardy (Boulogne and Calais), the last remaining English possessions in France, and these provided a profitable export trade in timber and fuel for these Sussex portsmen. The trade, however, was soon to go anyway for in Mary Tudor's reign (1553–8) England lost Calais, which cut off the supply of cannon from Calais—but released charcoal fuel for gun-casting in the Sussex Weald.

This Wealden ironmaking seems to have brought a pretty high rate of inflation. In 1539 Sussex iron cost from £5 to £7 per ton with £1 profit at the site. Ten years later it was up to £8 a ton at the forge, and £9½ in London, as its transport there cost 9/– a ton, due no doubt to the awful roads.

In Elizabeth's reign ironmaking expanded enormously and there was a large overseas market—some of which was illegal—so of course there was much smuggling. In 1574 the famous lists were drawn up of 115 ironmasters to enquire into use of timber and other matters. A complaint had been made by Ralph Hogge of Buxted who it seems had the export monopoly of cannon against others who were exporting. This sounds a familiar complaint to us nowadays by those who like to corner markets or have a monopoly; even then some Englishmen did not appear to like competition! So the ironmasters were summoned to appear before the Privy Council to give bonds that no cannon would be exported without a Royal licence.

The warning and summoning were carried out by the Privy
Council messenger, Richard Pedley, who made a quite remarkable journey of 483 miles in 19 days throughout the late winter
in spite of the dreadful roads. Sharp frosts may well have
helped, though, for this was the beginning of the climatic
downturn to be known as the 'Little Ice Age'.

An extract from the log for our area is worth recording:

Feb. 23	West Hoathly, East Grinstead	21 miles
24	Hartfield, Ashurst, Maresfield	31
25	Maresfield, Buxted, Rotherfield	
	(3 visits)	31
26	Framfield	22
28	Mayfield	21
Mar. 4	Mayfield, Frant	23

But not all the ironmasters appeared to sign bonds; some
pleaded old age or difficulty of travelling. Some like Sir Thomas
Gresham, the great financial magnate and friend of the Queen,
whom we met earlier at Mayfield, neither appeared nor signed
any bond. In fact that very year he exported a hundred cannon to
the King of Denmark and paid a very low export tax, as it was
agreed by the Royal assessors that 'he was no common
merchant'.

Others, more humble, like John Blacket who owned
Gravetye, simply did not turn up or sign anything, and it is
perhaps significant that nothing was heard of the furnace for
some years afterwards.

On Ashdown Forest Newbridge, which by now had two
furnaces, was owned by Sir Henry Bowyer who was acting for
the Queen anyway so he did not appear; neither apparently did
Ralph Hogge who owned Old Forge (Maresfield parish). He
described himself as 'the quenes Maiesties gonnestone maker of
yron for the office of her Ma'ties ordinnance . . .' and of course it
was his original complaint that had caused the whole business.

After this flurry of activity ironworking in our part of the
Sussex Weald is a series of peaks and troughs governed by the
needs of war. In between many domestic items were made like
trivets and skillets, cooking pots and such things as apothe-
cary's mortars, and goffering for the frills of a mob cap. Most of
the forges and furnaces were quite simple structures, which

quickly fell into ruin, although they could be equally quickly repaired in times of crisis or the original site extended. The later furnaces at Pippingford on the Forest were probably built for Marlborough's wars in the early eighteenth century. The last actual ironmaking in our area seems to have been at the Gravetye furnace, which was still working in 1769, but had finished by 1787.

We come now to discuss what remains of this long-lasting industry. Inside houses, museums and churches are many surviving objects actually cast and forged in this part of the Weald. These are graveslabs—some are of course in the churchyards—and firebacks, and later in Queen Anne's reign firedogs. The designs of the firebacks are often very fine, and favourite patterns were that of a phoenix or biblical subjects like Esther, and after the Restoration in 1660 royal designs with prominent CR II cast on them. Cast-iron milestones were made, but not in any quantity and many were removed in 1940 when there was a possible threat of invasion. There used to be one marked 'London 37' half a mile north of King's Standing on the Hartfield Road on Ashdown Forest.

The best place to see all this in one fell swoop is without any doubt Anne of Cleves Museum at Lewes, and especially the well-designed and presented ironworking gallery done by a young assistant curator, Stella Bellen. Much of what you see there is from Ashdown and nearby parts of the High Weald, and in the small archaeological museum at West Hoathly is a 'bear', that is a lump of iron that was imperfectly smelted.

Out in the countryside are the still quite numerous former furnace and hammer ponds. Some are reed fringed and isolated; others have been transformed into ornamental lakes with often not far away the beautiful houses that the ironmasters either acquired or built for themselves.

On the landscape itself are sometimes seen the remains of the former bays or dams, now often hidden by a tangle of thick undergrowth; otherwise they may have been built up with stone or brick later, sometimes by famous landscape gardeners like Repton at Buckhurst Park in Withyham, to make a suitable lake for the spacious grounds of a mansion. Others have just disappeared, or been quarried away if they contained slag by county surveyors ever on the look-out for cheap material with

which to pave their roads. In the many Wealden streams, some
of which appear far too tiny to have ever driven waterwheels,
are still much iron slag and cinder.

Here and there inside the many woods on Wadhurst Clay can
be seen a kind of dimpled 'up and down' landscape. These are the
remains of the many minepits dug for ore, though the same pit
often produced clay for marling and later for bricks and tiles.
Some are full of water and make very useful troughs for thirsty
cattle.

On Ashdown Forest are still many pits once dug for ore, and
the remains of some of them are on the side of the valley below
the southern edge of the Crowborough road at Nutley. The
nearby farm now called Marlpitts was once named Minepits
Farm, a faint reminder of the old ironworking days.

For the reader who is interested in seeing some of these relics,
once again the problem is that much that is worth seeing is on
private property, and of course not marked in any way. But here
I will record a selection of sites with interesting histories that I
know by personal experience, and of which I can safely say are
all on or near public footpaths or bridleways, where one can
'pass freely without let or hindrance' as our passports ever
hopefully request. They are all, plus some others, in the
Appendix with O.S. map references.

Starting with the northern slopes beyond the Forest there is
Gravetye, already mentioned, with its fine Tudor mansion
actually built in 1598 by an ironmaster named Infield. Further
downstream on this Medway headwater and reached by footpaths from Gravetye Woods is Mill Place, another fine ironmaster's house with ivy-covered Tudor chimneys built of stone
and hung tiles and now a farmhouse.

Along the Medway itself is Lower Parrock (with access by a
footpath from Upper Parrock), a very early forge (1513) and
furnace (1519) with an interesting and at times extraordinary
history. In 1513 the forgemaster, Robert Scorer, supplied 9 tons
of gunstones (cannon balls) to Henry VIII and in 1515 some to
the ship *Mary and John*—did he, one wonders, supply some to
the new *Mary Rose* built in 1520, and raised so dramatically in
1982?

Later the whole area, about 40 acres, was leased to Denise
Bowyer, an ironmaster's widow, who was forcibly evicted with

her workmen when the property changed hands through a chancery suit. However, she got her staff together and attacked the new owner's men and oxen with great vigour, literally to get her own back. The result of all this is unknown, but Denise was the mother of Sir Henry Bowyer, the ironfounder who managed Queen Elizabeth's affairs on Ashdown Forest.

Then in 1590 one Elliot took stone from Ashdown Forest without a licence to the furnace. And also at the site at one time was a flourishing pottery kiln worked by a skilled French potter. Eventually it seems that the site was overwhelmed by the Medway floods—quite a history for one place. On top of the hill overlooking the river is the beautiful fifteenth-century Hall-house of Upper Parrock, lived in at one time by one of the ironmasters. I found cinder and slag near a rather ragged wheatfield that must be chock-full of it, and a large lump of ironstone rests against a railway sleeper near the farm entrance, unconsciously a reminder of two former iron activities—now both gone.

Further down in a side valley the Hamsell Stream flows swiftly from the Forest, and across the level crossing west of Eridge Station is a spillway. This is from the old Birchden Forge near Harrison's rocks, that makes a grand little waterfall when the stream is full from Ashdown rain. Mr Norman Trepte, the present owner of Forge Farm, very kindly showed me over this fine building cleverly converted and restored from three original cottages by the people who now live at Hugget's Furnace Farm, south of Rotherfield, and told me how the forge leat flows in a culvert under the house—it once cooled the dairy—and out over the fields to the Hamsell Stream. The forge and its furnace at Hamsell, now a very fine ornamental lake which can be peeped at through the trees from a footpath, were important for tradition has it that the first Sussex ordnance (built-up mortars, not cast cannon) were made there. A later ironmaster, Robert Baker, was not a very good businessman and became bankrupt in 1708 in spite of having sixty-nine guns at two wharves on the Thames.

Westwards from Ashdown Forest amid the beautiful wooded slopes are three splendid large lakes, all ex-furnace ponds on western headwaters of the River Ouse.

The first at Strudgate is quite remote down a lane, opposite

Stoney Lane from the B2036, and surrounded by superb woods with some very large fine beech trees and Douglas firs. In the 1930s when Lord Cowdray owned Paddockhurst further north, water from this pond was used to drive turbines that pumped water from a spring up to the house. Hydraulic rams at Three-point Wood in Paddockhurst Park also pushed water to other parts of the Cowdray estate, but all of this little hydraulic enterprise is long since in ruins, and water comes from the more prosaic but no doubt efficient mains supply.

The second furnace pond is at Horsted Keynes, once famous for nailmaking, and is down a lane from the church. Here I found a beautiful piece of slag that could pass for an exotic mineral specimen. An interesting contemporary glimpse of the furnace working here is given by the Reverend Giles Moore of Horsted Keynes in his account book (1656–79): 'Payed to James Cripps for a plate cast for my kitchen chimney, besides two shillings given to the founders for casting, 13s.'

The third is at Sheffield Mill, also down a lane—a very long one from Furner's Green. I must admit I used a bike, but the journey is worth the effort as this large sheet of water has many waterfowl and is set among the trees of Sheffield Forest. You can also reflect on the unfortunate Admiral Lord Seymour who once owned it and the religious controversy that caused him to lose it.

Southwards from the Forest in rather different countryside on two tributaries of the Ouse, sometimes called the Uckfield River or Uckfield Water, are two sites of quite different aspect and interest. The first is at New Place Farm, south from Framfield down a side road from the B2101, where the furnace was of obscure origin, but the pond has been carefully trans-formed into a superbly landscaped ornamental lake and water garden surrounded by white and red rhododendrons, yellow azaleas and kingcups in the water and a background of trees including junipers and copper beeches. I saw it in late May and it looked very beautiful indeed.

The other site in north of Framfield, along a side road also off the B2102, at Pounsley and actually listed by the Department of the Environment as an ancient monument, but not marked on the ground of course at all. It is near a footpath, but quite difficult to see, but once you are there it is a tranquil reminder of an old industry, and I found a nice piece of slag in the bright reddish-brown-coloured stream and its little shingle bed, below the furnace bay which is preserved; the whole effect is very pleasant.

Finally eastwards from the Forest in the ridge and vale country are some sites in what was once the heart of the industry, some being of unusual historic interest. We can begin with Mayfield where in the High Street on a plinth is a cannon restored in 1977 by the local Historical Society. It was cast at the Mayfield furnace about 1660 by the Baker family, and for an instrument of war that has never fired an angry shot it has since had quite an eventful life. In 1824 it was dug out of the woods near the furnace by the old Tunbridge Wells road, and put on top of the porch of the former Archbishop's Palace—then a forlorn ruin. Later when the Palace was restored and became a Roman Catholic convent it was transferred inside to rest alongside St Dunstan's tongs—those of course by which he held the Devil's nose—and there it lay until recently.

The furnace was owned at one time in 1574 by Sir Thomas Gresham, whom we met a few pages back, and was but one of his many properties and in his time was used exclusively for the 'makeinge of Ordnance and Shott'. It was situated on a head-stream of the Upper Rother which lies in a steep little pic-turesque valley north of Mayfield; there is nothing to see now except a pleasant walk, but do not go along the road between 5 and 6 p.m. for it becomes a nightmare of fast commuter traffic that cares not for life or limb.

There are many forge and furnace sites within the Wadhurst area, but they seem to be on very private property, rather difficult of access and—naturally—not marked.

There are two fine Tudor houses both close to headwaters of the Kentish River Teise, one of which can easily be seen, the other only glimpsed. The splendid house called Lightlands, built in 1541 by a very rich ironmaster, Nicholas Fowle of Mayfield, was mentioned in Chapter 7 on account of its connection with Ashdown Forest. This can be viewed from two footpaths both off the A267 south of Frant. If you then continue along the footpath north of Lightlands passing through a wood you will arrive at a narrow side road south from the B2099 Wadhurst road. A short way still southwards brings you to Riverhall, where there was a forge and furnace. The lower pond still exists as does the bay; the mansion was rebuilt also by Nicholas Fowle in 1591, but is now much altered—mainly eighteenth century—but still with Elizabethan star chimneys. The modern owners (it seems to be in flats) discourage visitors by obscuring the public footpath notice near the entrance.

Hugget's Furnace Farm we came across earlier in the book, but the fine medieval house was later an ironmaster's. There is a great deal of mystery about who lived there and where exactly the furnace was, which by tradition cast the first cannon in 1543 here hence the oft-quoted rhyme: 'Master Hugget and his man John, they did cast the first Can-non.' However, Mr Jim Foster, the farmer from the neighbouring Hugget's Furnace Mill Farm, kindly showed me the stream banks (it is a tributary of the Uckfield Ouse) that were full of ironstone, probably exposed by the stream cutting down, for we are on actually the Ashdown Beds just here. Still I have two fine pieces of glass slag to show that at least a furnace was somewhere nearby.

Mr Foster also told me of two interesting incidents of some years before. The first was when Ernest Straker visited the farm, and Mr Foster was a lad of thirteen or fourteen. I asked him what the famous researcher was like: 'Somewhat obstinate,' said Mr Foster, 'He insisted that things ought to be in a certain place, irrespective of other circumstances.'

The second some years later was when suddenly down the lane appeared a London taxi, out of which jumped an excited American named Huggett. He had, it seems, been on a visit to Europe and wished to see the 'ancestral home' of the Hugget family—there are apparently a number of Huggett societies in the U.S.A. He was in a great hurry and had nothing to remind him of his English ancestry, so Mr Foster very kindly gave him a cannon ball that had been found on the farm and mounted; at which the highly delighted American departed in his taxi.

At this point we can speculate a little on who actually cast the first cannon and where in 1543. There are possibly four furnaces which may have that honour, if indeed honour it be; one is on Ashdown Forest and three close to it. They are: Oldlands owned and worked by Parson Levett; then under a mile to the south Hendall owned by the famous Pelham family and worked by four Frenchmen (afterwards the Pope family whose family manor is still there nearby); then within the Forest Marshalls owned by Ralph Hogge; and finally in Buxted itself at Iron Plat just north of where the station now stands. Straker thought this was too small for making cannon, but as later researchers have found he could be wrong sometimes.

After actual ironmaking ceased in the Weald, the local black-smith came into his own, as we saw earlier, but small iron foundries were set up in various towns, especially during the nineteenth century. In Lewes for example there was the famous Phoenix Ironworks which lasted well into the twentieth cen-tury; and Tonbridge in Kent actually made their own bridge across the Medway.

But it was out in the countryside in the small villages of Sussex that the blacksmith often became a real local craftsman, and his fame sometimes spread to the cricket field where powerful arms helped to make demon bowlers and slogging batsmen.

For some hundreds of years these craftsmen continued their trade into the 1930s when first the motor car and later the farm tractor plus the increasing amount of mechanized equipment reduced the need for their individual skills and services. Many of the forges thus became garages, as the one at Nutley on the Forest did, no doubt helped by the main Eastbourne road being diverted through Nutley instead of going through Chelwood Gate.

Appropriately enough, I suppose, it was in the old ironmaking centre of Wadhurst that I met the most interesting blacksmith, Mr Bassett, whose family have been carrying on smithy work for over eighty years. He himself had been there for sixty of these, serving as a volunteer fireman for forty-five years and living in the same house for over forty years. Talking to him was living social history and his many varied reminiscences covered much time and space. He had many sharp and clear memories of such events as the Atora Beef Suet advertising van drawn by oxen in the 1920s; then the unusual job of trimming the feet of the four pedigree Ayrshire bulls that Lord Abergavenny had out at Mark Cross, and in the last war the very long weary hours of work on tanks, carriers and trailers for the local Ministry of Transport depot.

His father, a blacksmith who had died aged ninety-two, had handled much work for Sussex coachbuilders which lasted into the early 1930s, and he remembered a certain Mr Skinner, a sheet-iron expert who worked for them and was a real specialist at 'fire welding'. This, said Mr Bassett, was far stronger than spot welding—'You couldn't draw it asunder,' he added with emphasis. And all through this long period the usual smithy work went on of making and repairing tools, handles, hoes, axes, billhooks, shoeing horses of course and the very important plough repairs—especially the many different types in use in various counties like the Sussex Pratt draw plough. Later I had the privilege of watching Mr Bassett forging horseshoes—mild steel, not iron, as this once common product now seems to be in short supply.

In Horsted Keynes, by contrast, I talked to an interesting modern blacksmith, Mr Hoare-Ward, who admitted to having been in the village a mere ten years; he was a specialist in ornamental ironwork and gates, but took on what he called 'potboiler work' like commercial netting. His complaint was the same as Mr Bassett's—the problem of getting iron now, and having to make do with mild steel, but he was a cheerful and contented man who obviously enjoyed his work.

10

Ashdown Forest Today and Tomorrow?

The administration of the Forest today, in common with that of other organizations, has become larger and more complex, and although basically the Conservators function as they were intended to by the 1885 Act, outside changes and pressures have brought further Acts and more control from beyond, both locally and within the county.

The Board of Conservators now consists of sixteen members, eleven of whom are appointed and five who are elected Commoners. One member represents the Lord of the Manor, Earl de la Warr; eight are from East Sussex County Council at Lewes; and two from the Wealden District Council at Crowborough. One of the elected Commoners is Chairman of the Board—Mr G. H. Wills of Coleman's Hatch.

To assist the Board as Clerk to the Conservators and as Forest Superintendent is Lieutenant-Commander Peter Angell D.S.C. and his Deputy-Superintendent is Mr Peter Donnelly, appointed in 1982. The staff also has a Secretary-Bookkeeper, Mrs Janet Ruxton, and four Forest Rangers: Len Arnold, John Linton, Dick Montague, and Jonathan Pedder, who are each responsible for a quarter of the Forest. These sections are called Chases, reviving an old Forest term. There are also two permanent workmen and sixteen people employed under the Manpower Services Commission as well as several voluntary rangers and information staff.

The new headquarters of the Administration is the Ashdown Forest Centre at Broadstone Warren near the old Rangers Depot along the Wych Cross to Coleman's Hatch road. This is a remarkable group of buildings, incorporating the frames of three old Sussex barns, and most of it has been built by the Forest staff themselves, using Manpower Services Commission labour too and a great deal of voluntary help supervised by the Rangers. The roof was thatched with heather from the Forest, and the cost has been met by an Appeal fund and grant aid from the Countryside Commission.

The Centre has three functions: first as a Rangers' Depot; second as the Conservators' Office; and third as an Information Centre. The last function is low key—to inform, but not to attract custom.

Financing of the Administration is somewhat complex. Originally it was from an annual rate levied upon each Commoner, but now in addition there is support from the District and County Councils, plus grants from the Countryside Commission, together with labour provided by the Youth Opportunities Programme.

The year 1982 was in some way one of controversy on the Forest, so we will examine opinions, and reserve comment for later.

I had a most interesting conversation with the Forest Superintendent, Peter Angell, and what I learnt is as follows. He told me that in general the Commoners had a protective attitude towards their Forest, but of the 650 registered only a mere handful still used their rights of common to graze and to collect estovers of birch, willow and alder. Only one (elderly) Commoner from Prickett's Hatch still regularly cuts bracken on the Forest for litter. Many had lost their rights of common for failing to register under the 1965 Act (for the registration of all common land in England). Peter Angell thought that one of the basic problems underlying all aspects of life on Ashdown was simply that there were no longer any real countrymen, and that many Commoners lived in the now rather suburbanized Forest Row. This is a statement that few I would think could possibly dispute; it is a simple fact of life in our highly urbanized society.

This brought up the question of visitors, some 1½ million yearly, and I asked him what he thought were the main reasons that brought people to the Forest. The heaviest month was May, which rather surprised me, but of course it is a factor of climate; the Forest can often be at its best in late spring when the views are superb. This is one of the main reasons people come. For example, from Gills Lap it is possible on a clear day to see from the North to the South Downs, a distance of forty miles. Otherwise many visitors just like to park their cars and stroll about near the car parks.

These are a very controversial subject, but the Board has a definite policy regarding them. Many now have hard standing and others are grassed areas which can be controlled or closed at any time, especially in the summer. They are paved with Kentish Rag as it is hard wearing, blends with the surroundings and of course does not have to be brought too far. Whenever possible the parks are screened and landscaped and the Conservators feel that this is a better method of dealing with the huge influx of car-borne visitors than the old pattern of just pulling off the road anywhere and everywhere. Of course the visitors brought litter, and as large bins are unsightly most of it has to be buried.

He said the Conservators were apprehensive at the loss of heather and wet heath, and at the encroaching of pine and birch which would of course obscure the views.

I then rather tentatively broached the emotive subject of horseriding, which is largely controlled by permits, but there is a certain amount of illegal riding, especially on footpaths. If caught culprits had their permits removed, but Peter Angell added that with the colossal rise in horseriding during the last fifteen years it was a very difficult task to have complete control over all riders. There are two riding centres on the Forest: Henry Osborne's Trekking Centre at Misbourne Farm and stables at White House Farm, Duddleswell; and two just outside, at Marsh Green and another Trekking centre at Chelwood Gate.

I enquired about wildlife, especially the fallow deer which are in the enclosures and come in from the fringes. Many are killed on the Forest roads, usually at night by accident, sometimes by sheer carelessness on the part of the drivers, and about fifty deer succumb to these hazards each year. There are still plenty of adders of course, which we shall discuss later, and badgers it seems were actually on the increase, as their cover is becoming denser.

The actual area of commons is increasing by small purchases of land. For example, 86 acres have been added in the last two years, the most recent being 11 acres at Braeberry Hatch, Chelwood Gate, which adjoins land previously bought.

I raised the question of the Radio Station at Duddleswell Crossroads and I was told that although part of the Diplomatic Wireless Service its priorities were much less than hitherto, and it was eventually moving to a site on the Suffolk coast, so the land would be recovered.

These were the main points which we discussed, and Lieutenant-Commander Angell was frank and clear in all his answers, and my personal impression was that he had a difficult job to do, and was carrying it out very ably.

Of course to find out what people think about a situation, especially if it is at all controversial, the only way is to talk to them in their own environment and when they are at ease. This is what I felt would give me some inside knowledge of the Forest and its problems; there would be many different views, but in total would at least give a picture of the existing state of affairs, and might even provide a lead for the future.

As the area was once a real forest and as trees are important at any time, I went therefore to see John Gent, an appointed member of the Board and in charge of its Riding Committee, and a trained forester working for English Woodlands. He lives at Campfield Rough on the Forest—the name is from a Mr Campfield and nothing to do with camps—in a house with a magnificent view southwards over the Forest towards the distant South Downs, once again underlining one of the features that makes the Forest so popular. John Gent was a forthright man and not afraid to expound his views on national policy towards the countryside and the scaling down of the Forestry Commission's personnel and privatization of forests due to economy cuts. He thought that the withdrawal of the Grey Squirrel Bounty by the Government had made a desperately serious situation regarding forestry (grey squirrels damage mature trees in winter).

We talked about one of the old enclosed parts of the Forest, Five Hundred Acre Wood owned by Earl de la Warr, which is now mainly conifers on the poor sandy soils, Corsican and Scots pine with chestnut coppice. This type of woodland can be easily thinned, saving labour. He said that most softwood planting had ceased in the 1970s.

Regarding the Forest Mr. Gent said it was a different landscape from the 1920s when it was fairly heavily grazed, and by 1945 there was a certain amount of oak coppice; now 80 per cent of the Forest was reverting to oak-birch scrub woodland, and the present open landscape of the Forest was a fire climax vegetation, that is its natural condition was altered by centuries of intermittent burning instead of natural growth, on a large scale, which is essentially a modern phenomenon and must eventually revert to oak scrub.

After seeing John Gent I thought of how small Britain's woodland is by comparison with that of our European neighbours. Our total is 9 per cent, and if you remove Sussex and Scotland the average per county is very small. By comparison West Germany has 30 per cent, France has 25 per cent, and, surprisingly, Italy, which is not normally thought of as a land of forests, has 27 per cent.

Of course the nature of the Forest landscape is all important to the few Commoners who still graze their animals on the open areas, so I went down to Londonderry Farm in the Millbrook valley. This is a small 20-acre holding farmed by Mrs Anne Sheldrick, an elected Commoner who grazes her twenty-five Jacob and Jacob Crossbred ewes on the Forest in the autumn, after the lambs have been weaned. She has a problem with her stock in that they might stray on to the nearby A22 over the other side of the Millbrook stream. This problem is being tackled by a survey of the possibility of putting cattle grids on the Forest roads. Mrs Sheldrick is also in charge of the Vegetation Management Committee on the Board, and is an ecologist and environmentalist; and one of the first things she said was: 'Ashdown Forest is not a Country Park!' She pointed out to me that one of the major problems of the Forest is maintaining the balance between woodland and open ground. Conservation work has been concentrated on keeping the main areas of wet and dry heath open, mainly by cutting out young birch and Scots pine (these of course regenerate naturally). This was a difficult task needing much labour, and some good work had been done with Ranger Linton and volunteer help. Bracken was an eternal problem, and the older heather is degenerating.

Anne Sheldrick said that the Forest Management Plan was to have a vegetation map of the various species on Ashdown, for you cannot preserve until you know what you have got to preserve, and plant identification is all important. She was as good as her word and took me out on to the open heathland and showed me the Common Sundew (*Drosera rotundifolia*). This is a typical plant of the wet heath and moors, which grows on mosses and even bare peat, but it is very small—although once you spot the neat rosette of round red leaves, and in the summer its small white five-petalled flower rising up from the rosette, you realize it is conspicuous by its unusual appearance.

To see what Forest dwellers of long standing felt about modern Ashdown I went along to see the Seymour family at New Pond Cottages on enclosed land at the south-eastern side of the Forest near the old Crowborough Gate on the present A26 Uckfield Road. I have mentioned Mrs Seymour earlier; she is a most interesting old lady, whose husband had farmed for fifty-three years at Crabtree Farm, a 60-acre holding behind the cottages on the slopes of the hill running down from King's Standing. She and her son felt strongly that some of the bridleways were overused—'There are far too many horses,' they said. This had spoilt flowers like gentians and disturbed bird life, like the habitats of curlews which they had remembered, but now no longer seen or heard. I asked her daughter-in-law about her part of the Forest, St John's Common. She was a dark-haired girl, born in one of the old hamlets that now make up Crowborough, and rather disturbed by developments taking place nowadays. One thing the Seymours were in favour of, probably like many older families on the Forest, was controlled burning of the heathland; this is an old, traditional practice with a long history on the Forest.

After I left the Seymours I had a practical demonstration of what can happen if you stray from the path on the Forest in summertime when the bracken is high, for I completely lost my way, and it was twilight before I regained the Crowborough road. I wandered about and hacked my way through bracken, scrub and an undergrowth of tangled brambles.

Pippingford Park has been mentioned earlier, when I have traced its history, but as the present owner, Alan Morriss, has always allowed me free use of his land and knowing his ideas and hopes for its eventual conversion into some kind of Nature Reserve I have explored the estate fairly thoroughly. For financial reasons he has had to lease out part to the Army, and the chain of ponds and lakes to fishermen—but the latter he told me were rather untidy with their litter, and the Army far cleaner. He has introduced Phragmites reeds on to the ponds, and felt that there was not actually a great variety of fish, and in fact this is true of most English rivers. He has a great interest in all kinds of wildlife, especially insects, and told me that seven years previously he released butterflies he had obtained from a butterfly farm at Ashford, and that the White Admiral was now flourishing with their larvae feeding here on honeysuckle. One day I was shown the wing of a Purple Emperor which he had literally found on his doorstep.

When I met him some two years before he had been nursing a sick buzzard; now he said they were quite common, and that also there were plenty of Canada geese here; they originally had been migrants, then they became ornamental waterfowl, and now are the only inland breeding wild geese, having colonized flooded gravel pits.

One afternoon in late July wandering about I saw, close to, a fallow deer and her fawn, dragonflies on a small pond with a solitary red water lily, and a green woodpecker; and as I returned past the decayed splendour of the house with its views from the mossy steps I thought that Pippingford with its sandy sterile soils should never be anything other than Nature intended.

In contrast to this estate, away down at the southern end of the Forest is Boringwheel House and its very fine lake. I was very kindly shown around by the owner, Mr Clive Impey, who has a trout-breeding station here. He has some impressive records for fish caught in the large and beautiful lake; in 1979 a rainbow trout weighing 22 pounds 1 ounce and a brown trout at 17 pounds 12 ounces were taken. These breeding ponds are an interesting modern version of the medieval stew ponds, but Mr Impey has also another interest in that he has laid out a golf course, which took him ten years to complete.

The day I talked to him the torrential rains of July had just caused the waters of the Ouse headstream that flows through the lake to destroy the massive spillway, which had been very solidly constructed of sandstone blocks a century earlier. Mr Impey told me that replacement costs would run into thousands of pounds but that when rebuilding he might install a small turbine to generate his own power; immediately my thoughts went to what Mr Newnham at Cross-in-Hand had said about using our streams for water power.

Clive Impey went on to recount rather amusingly some of the disputes he had with two local Forest people who had been quite recalcitrant, but one old farmer had said to him, without malice, the old Forest maxim: 'You'll soon learn to cut your hedges from the inside!' However, my impression of Boringwheel was that the owner was a generous man, knowledgeable and a good man to have on the Forest.

From Boringwheel I went back again to the far northern edge at Newbridge, where on a 20-acre small-holding within the Forest I met and talked with Tom Philcox, a Sussex man, who turned out to be very interesting indeed. His family had been in Hartfield two hundred years, Sussex enough in all conscience, but they were originally from north Norfolk. What, I wondered, had brought the original Philcox such a long way (as it must have been then) from his home ground? Then I recalled that it was in Norfolk where the great agricultural revolution had started with big efficient estates coming into being with enclosures and the disappearance of many commons. Ashdown in the rural, isolated Sussex Weald would offer hope for a small farmer.

But in the twentieth century Tom Philcox had travelled as well, managing farms in Devon, and had brought back a Devon wife to Newbridge. Here he fitted into the pattern as though he had never left it, and was running fifteen sheep on land that had hungry soils, and drained well—far too well in fact—and as he said: 'doing my own dog work'; he whistled as he spoke and the sheep came towards him.

He told me about the Hartfield families of long standing: Elliott the butcher, the Medhursts, Killick among others, and how village life had changed so dramatically after centuries of an almost unchanging rhythmic rurality to a commuter pattern now, even among villagers. Newbridge still has an air of settled rurality, probably because the ancient ironworking left behind features that add to the charm of the landscape: the hammer pond, water channels, scattered cottages and a field pattern that goes back to South Saxon enclosure of nearly a thousand years ago.

The only village of any size on the Forest is Nutley, whose growth has been linear, beginning from the medieval waste edge below the level of the road, and gradually becoming in more modern times a line of dwellings along the highway itself. Later building made little enclaves from this pattern, like Hillend Close, where a group of six council houses with vernacular hung tiles and hedges fit in compactly and neatly.

Today the village, whose site commands a fine view over the open heathland, has lost some of its attraction because of the constant fast and heavy traffic along the A22, which sooner or later reduces all main-road villages to the equivalent of an American whistle-stop tour. This must affect the village life, with the danger that it may lose its contact with the Forest, although it is too small, thankfully, to become like Crow-borough; but it is a far cry from the poverty and loneliness when the landlord of an inn here would buy you a drink if you just stopped and talked to him.

Rather different in character over on the south-eastern corner is the relatively modern village of Fairwarp, which is much quieter and whose life seems more bound up with the Forest; and where the first nature reserve on the Forest is situated. This is a triangle of land bordering Nursery Lane, Marlpits Lane and the road to the village, an area of about 8½ acres which was established in April 1981 after being cleared of scrub. It is cared for in its natural state with little disturbance of its wildlife by a Voluntary Warden, the naturalist Brian Hoath. Some control over the woodland has to be maintained to allow light to penetrate so that some plants like catmint and foxglove can flourish, giving habitats for birds and insects; and nesting boxes are provided to help birds like blue tits, spotted flycatchers and nuthatches. One feature which I thought was very enterprising was the transference of wild plants, like the rare Butchers Broom (*Ruscus aculeatus*), an evergreen with tiny white flowers, from its vulnerable site; I have never seen this on the

Forest but I remember it years ago in Devon.

Officially the Forest is classed as an A.N.O.B. (Area of Outstanding Natural Beauty) and also an S.S.S.I. (Site of Special Scientific Interest), but it is perhaps slightly ironic to realize that the old Royal Forests by their very nature protected much wildlife and plants, so that today their sites are still sources of rare plants and animals, like the New Forest, Epping and here on Ashdown.

Where plants are concerned recognition is vital, and the Forest is practically the only place in Sussex where the Marsh Gentian (*Genista pneumonanthe*) is found. It is a damp or wet heath species, and even before the war it was reckoned as rare or locally frequent on the Forest at places like the bog near Chelwood Gate, and between Pippingford and Nutley, and Crowborough and Wych Cross. It is easy to recognize with its bright-blue trumpet flower, and delicate green stripes on the outside, and is about 1–1½ inches long.

Many of the dry heath plants are becoming rarer. Three that under fifty years ago were common were Saw Wort or Needle Furze (*Serratula tinctoria*), Petty Whin (*Genista anglica*) and the Creeping Willow (*Salix repens*). The Saw Wort has purple flowers, Petty Whin yellow or orange spikes, and Creeping Willow's yellow catkins are like most other willows, but its creeping stems make it recognizable.

Down in the alder carrs and similar areas Bog Bean (*Menyanthes trifolia*) was once very common; by the 1930s it was just occasional and found abundantly at Coleman's Hatch, Crow's Nest and Camp Hill; but by 1967 it was restricted to only three sites. Apparently this was because it had been gathered as a medicinal plant for blood purifying and rheumatism; but it may have recovered for the *Sussex Naturalist Book* now says it is again occasional, but only on the Forest. The flowers are spiky pink and white which poke above fresh water or marsh, so it is fairly easy to spot; and as nowadays rheumatism is eased by more sophisticated methods the plant may have a less troubled future.

Along the woodland streams you may find the Bog Pimpernel (*Anagallis tenella*) with its pink delicate flowers which open in the sun; but it is much reduced now, although once it was found near Forest Row, Chuck and Coleman's Hatches. The Ivy-leaved Bellflower (*Wahlenbergia hederacea*) I had never seen until I found one near a brook in Pippingford; but I am told it is not quite so rare now as fifteen years ago. You can easily tread on it, which would be a pity for with its pale-blue flowers it is one of the most charming of the Bellflower family including the Harebell.

However, the really rare plants are the ferns that grow in what is called poor fern like the Marsh and Beech varieties, once abundant on Ashdown in the nineteenth century.

Finally, often Forest plants reappear later after having been repeatedly reported as extinct following heath fires; an example is the rare Hairy Greenweed (*Genista pilosa*) which has been seen at Gills Lap. Another is the rare Bog Orchid (*Malaxis paludosa*) which has tiny yellow-green flowers and is very small (2 inches high) and not easily seen. This was classed as extinct, but found near Fairwarp in 1952, and recently in a redundant tank trap on the Forest. But others, sadly, are really gone like the Small White Orchid, not seen for thirty years.

We come now to birds, and as my own sightings and recognition are fairly limited, I say quite openly that what follows is mainly due to the expert knowledge and kindness of Mr J. Houghton of the Sussex Ornithological Society; some of these comments also apply to areas on the fringes of the Forest, particularly where they are well wooded.

The Forest is well known as an interesting place for bird-watching, and we can begin with the summer migrants like the Tree Pipit, which even I recognized with its parachute flight down into trees. Next is the Redstart, often seen in old beech trees like those at Broadstone Warren, and then the Wood Warbler found in birch copses, and identified by its yellow throat and white belly. Its cousin the Garden Warbler is often found in coppiced chestnuts, more probably within the enclosed margins than on the Forest itself. In other wooded areas you may hear the Blackcap with its mellow and rich song, and see it with its glossy black crown, and the Chiff-Chaff which I have often heard, but only once recognized as it always seems so much like other warblers. In the scrub you can often see the Whitethroat, a chattering bird and easily identified (as its name implies).

In young conifers and grass you may hear the distinctive note of the Grasshopper Warbler, who makes a noise like an angler reeling in, and in the boggy grass around Misbourne you hear, rather than see, the secretive Snipe, although I have sometimes seen them. Out on the open heathland, where the parts are less burnt, you might see and hear the rarer Woodlark, whose song is even more melodious than its much commoner cousin the Skylark.

One interesting summer visitor is the Nightjar, who appears after May with the unmistakable 'churring' rising and falling sustained song. Fires have sometimes destroyed their habitats, but Ashdown is still the best place in the county to hear him; seeing him with his 'dead leaf' camouflage is rarer.

Other partial migrants are the Buntings: the familiar Yellowhammer, although apart from Horney Common (where a correspondent to the Forest Newsletter, Madeleine Reader, says that she has seen them throughout the year) the place I have seen many was along the old railway track between Forest Row and Hartfield. The other, the Reed Bunting, is a winter migrant, like the Redpoll, and seen in great flocks. Whilst floundering around in an alder carr I once saw a Redpoll with its red forehead and pink breast; but I did not know then that alder carrs are one of their haunts.

Much rarer is the Stonechat—down to ten pairs in 1964 but it has now recovered to reach sixty or so. Another is the Curlew, familiar enough to those who know the uplands and moors further north, but rare in the south-east; some have been seen at Weir Wood, and they have bred on the Forest since 1932, but I have seen only a few since 1948 when walking on the Forest.

Three other winter migrants are finches: the Siskin, found near the Wych Cross and Nutley fruit farms, the Crossbill (a bird of the conifers and so dependent on food supply) and the Brambling which likes beechmast. Two others, thrushes, are the Redwing and Fieldfare, but they are more likely to be seen in cultivated areas, perhaps in the south of the Forest. Finally of course are the resident Tits; apart from the common three, there are the Marsh and the Willow, the latter noted for its nightingale-like song—the Nightingale alas! is no longer a summer visitor to Ashdown.

When we come to birds of prey I am on surer ground, probably because I have seen more of them. Two that are often seen on the

Forest are the Sparrowhawk, in wooded country with its cruising flight at hedge level, and out in the open the Kestrel with its rapid hovering flight and often perching on the odd isolated clump. Two rarer birds are the Red-backed Shrike, which has a habit of impaling its prey on thorn bush 'larders', so we are not surprised to find it in the Isle of Thorns, and the other—the Hobby—if seen at all is in the Scots pine clumps. In the winter you might see the rare Hen Harrier (so often the victim of gamekeepers) for there are three pairs on the Forest; and the Grey Shrike is an occasional visitor.

Of owls, the Little Owl is seen here in summer; the Barn Owl is an 'accidental' and prefers more urbanized areas, whilst the most common is the Tawny Owl, a large bird frequently heard with its deep musical hooting on all parts of the Forest. And to end this survey, that elegant marsh bird, the Grey Heron, is seen at Braeberry Hatch, and I have seen a number at Pippingford.

From birds to mammals, most of which are nocturnal so their presence is more often known by their tracks in mud, snow or dust, and usually we can only glimpse them. They are not normally as popular as birds—presumably because birds are considered more beautiful—which is a pity because mammals are interesting and intelligent. On the Forest the largest and most common are the Deer, usually Fallow with dappled coats and the buck's broad antlers. They are great jumpers and very agile. Much rarer is the larger Red Deer, which prefers woodland. And the smallest are the Roe Deer, again rare; they are active animals and good swimmers, not that any of the Forest streams are wide or deep enough to act as barriers, but it was once thought that the electrified railway line between London and Brighton might be one. However, they pass through the woods above Balcombe Tunnel.

The Deer sometimes present a task for the Rangers who may be called out at all hours if one is injured or killed by traffic on the Forest roads, and then they are humanely shot; but thankfully some of the injured ones can be nursed back to health.

Now to the Fox, usually a night raider, who often lives in other people's burrows and whose den has always many entrances and exits, and an emotional subject like the horse-rider. Foxes are on the increase here, although I have seen only one on Ashdown, a vixen on enclosed land at the Pheasantry; but I have seen others on the fringes, at Summerford by the Medway and at Town Row, Rotherfield. Two hunts used the Forest (I believe combined now): the Eridge, and the Surrey and Old Burstow. The Eridge are at the Abergavenny Estate, the Nevills being a great hunting family—the 2nd Marquess was killed aged eighty-five in January 1938 when his horse stumbled at a children's meet.

To those who want to abolish foxhunting on the Forest, one can say only two things: first, it has been a traditional hunting ground since being enclosed in the thirteenth century, and secondly it all depends on whether you keep chickens!

Another large mammal is the Badger, unmistakably marked, again nocturnal, and capable of making a great variety of noises. I have heard him growling and snorting at night whilst I was walking about beyond Greenwood Gate Clump.

But most of the Forest's mammals are small, like the two shrews: Common and Pygmy, the latter being a very old inhabitant, and here well before the Ice Ages. Both shrews have the same habits, swim well and are active both day and night, except that you are more likely to see the Pygmy Shrew amongst the dry grass and shrubs, whilst the Common Shrew does not mind marshlands.

Water brings to mind two other good swimmers: the Stoat and the Water Vole. The Stoat is really an animal of the woods, unlike his small relative the Weasel which prefers sandy areas but near water; and he will often be seen scampering across roads on the Forest, his long slender sausage-like body moving very quickly.

The Water Vole (*Avicola amphibius*) is one of my favourite creatures and I have often watched them near river banks, being myself very fond of rivers (as I have followed a number of them from source to mouth, like the Medway in England and the Loire in France). Tramping along stream courses in the Forest I have sometimes waited after seeing an earth fall by the banks, and then sure enough a dark furry body with a long tail slides down into the water and swims away swiftly; it is not often realized that they can even dive and swim under ice.

And now finally, on to a most interesting group of mammals—

the Bats! Oh dear, you do not like them, they get in your hair and remind you of vampires and Dracula? Well, some live on or near the Forest, and they are highly protected as well, being insect eaters and not blood drinkers. The one you are most likely to see is the smallest European bat—the Pipistrelle (*P. pipistrellus*), which is very common and flies very fast over open country, sometimes during the day, but usually at early evening just after sunset, fairly high up and even during strong winds. Another you might see is the Long-eared Bat (*Pleocotus auritus*), but nearer to trees and bushes for he is a real night-flier and rather shy, being small except for his very long large ears.

Here we can mention their secret: bats use of course a form of echo-location to find their way—sonar rather than radar—the same method used for hunting submarines, except that they are in air not water, where the speed of sound is five times as great.

Another bat you might notice is the Whiskered Bat, literally moustachioed—his French name is Vespertillon à mous-taches—and he too is small and grey, and mainly a tree creature and slow flier, fluttering above water sometimes for the insects, often seen in the early evening and in the day as well.

The largest and rarest of all—in fact found only in Sussex out of the whole of Britain—is the Mouse-eared Bat, the largest European bat, another nightflier, which sometimes migrates over long distances. If you see one you should report the fact to the Sussex Naturalists Trust who will be greatly interested; he is large and once seen, unmistakable.

From bats to reptiles; and one of the commonest is the small lizard, often seen sunning itself on sandstone outcrops, but usually shy and liable to scurry at the sight and sound of humans.

And now to snakes, of which the Forest has all three native British species. We will begin with the rarest, the Smooth Snake or Coronella. These have suffered much from their super-ficial resemblance to adders as they can be brown, greyish or reddish. They were not recorded until 1859 (in the Bourne-mouth district) and were often killed mercilessly in the Hampshire sandy districts in mistake for adders—either way a stupid action. By 1973 they were classified as a greatly threat-ened species. They are interesting animals in that they kill their prey in constrictor fashion in the manner of their larger cousins overseas.

Next is one of the most beautifully coloured of all British native creatures: the Ringed or Grass Snake, often a brilliant green. This is quite common and can be easily tamed; in fact they can distinguish between different people, and will come to those they know. They can grow quite long, although the average is about 2 feet 2½ inches. The longest ever found was in Surrey at 6 feet 3 inches—a female. As usual with snakes, the female grass snake is longer. They are found far to the north of Britain in quite cool climates, like northern Sweden (65 N. Lat.). Some people are repelled by them, which is a pity, because they are harmless and indeed useful creatures, but one lady I knew in Nutley was frightened by one chasing a frog across her lawn—its natural prey.

The last, and most common, British snake is the Adder or Viper. First the origin of its name: the Saxon word was *snaca*, snake; and adder comes from *naedre* = Nadder, a creeping thing; it has gone into modern German as *Natter*. It also is in a place-name—Netherfield near Battle—from Nadderfeld, Adder's Field or open space. Adders are mainly distinguished by their dark zig-zag stripes or, in the case of black ones—for melanism is not uncommon—by a uniform stripe. (Black Adders are found in Wales, and there is a place-name in Lowland Scotland and a river name.) However, their ground colouring varies a great deal, and no two adders are completely alike. And to complicate matters they have sexual dimorphism, which is normally rare in snakes: the males can be creamy white, greyish, silvery with jet black stripes, and the females are reddish or golden.

They are common on Ashdown, and anyone who has seen their mating dance with the males wrestling has seen one of Nature's most interesting events. They are not large snakes—any adder over 2 feet is a big one and the biggest found recently (1971) in Sussex was 3 feet 2½ inches long; and the longest found on the Forest was at Crowborough, just short of 2 feet. There are a number of misconceptions about them. Although they love the sun, they do not like great heat, and they will be absent on a really hot day. They hibernate in October, do not make their own holes, sometimes being found with other hibernating creatures, even their prey. They are not a savage snake, in fact quite timid, and their chief enemy is MAN; others are hedgehogs, perhaps the badger and, in water, the ferocious pike and eels.

Now for those who may meet them on walks, and are unlucky enough or stupid enough to attack them and get bitten, there are some things you should NOT do. No potassium permanganate, no tourniquet (because amateur surgery can be worse than the bite), but an anti-histamine drug could be effective, whilst an anti-venom might not be. The best answer is to leave the timid and retiring adder alone. The bite is fatal only if it gets into the bloodstream.

I have seen perhaps a dozen in my life, in many varied places: Land's End, Exmoor, Medway headwaters, some on the Forest—one at Pippingford—and two in the Spanish Pyrenees. They are remarkably widespread and found up to 9,000 feet and above the Arctic Circle to 68° North.

Our last group of Ashdown wildlife is insects, and perhaps one extra reason for keeping the Forest wild is the butterflies; some are not seen elsewhere and many are more common there than outside the Forest. Many of them will be familiar to the older readers, for alas insecticides have polished off many varieties. Here are some: Comma, Brimstone, Small Copper, Gatekeeper (Hedge Brown), Tortoiseshell and Red Admiral. Near the Radio Station I have seen many small Blues, and two years ago Clouded Yellows in Pippingford. But the best person on the Forest to tell you about butterflies is Anne-Marie Montague, the wife of Ranger Dick Montague, who lives at Hillside Cottage, Duddleswell, and will tell you where butterflies are to be found.

Other insects are the Dragonflies and Demoiselle Flies already mentioned, and our last creatures of all look wild, but are very gentle indeed. These are the Highland Cattle bred by Mrs Linton, the Administrative Officer at the Radio Station, and I was very lucky to go inside and see them grazing and being fed. One is pure Highland and the daughter was crossbred with a Sussex. Ashdown is an ideal environment for them, a rough landscape like their native Scottish Highlands, and it is interesting that another 'wild' English landscape, Charnwood Forest in Leicestershire, developed on ancient rocks, has herds of these cattle.

If you are a good walker, you might wonder what would be good routes across the Forest. There are many, but one that combines the best of surrounding country and also the enclosed parts (not normally open to the public) as well as a good cross-section of the open Forest is the waymarked Wealdway Walk. Here my own experience might be helpful: I drove to Ashurst Station and left my vehicle there, and started out on a footpath which joins the Wealdway at Hale Court Farm. Incidentally, it was a field of wheat in July and halfway across the field I saw a Red Deer which looked rather strange in amongst the corn.

The walk then goes via Withyham and enters the Forest at Five Hundred Acre Wood, enclosed as long ago as 1693 and reminiscent of A. A. Milne's books. It then reaches Greenwood Gate clump, and goes across open heathland parallel with the B2188 to Camp Hill; then through Brown's Brook and enclosed piecemeal land by Oldlands Gate, then through Hendall Wood, which I mentioned earlier in the book (the name means Hind's valley, O.E. Hind-dael), and on to Five Ash Down.

For returning go on either to Uckfield or Buxted Stations; the railway journey back to Ashurst on an early summer evening is well worth doing, for you have a very fine distant view all the way, and not obscured by roads and urban clutter.

The other marked walk is the Vanguard Way from Forest Row, via Coleman's Hatch, Newbridge Splash, Gills Lap; then parallel with Old Lodge Road (B2026) to King's Standing, and down then up to Poundgate on the Crowborough Road (A26).

The very mixed and scattered community on and near the Forest of Commoners—small farmers, tradespeople, commuters, retired folk, and landowners—were often ill-informed about what is happening in their own area. Now they are served very well by a *Newsletter*, started in 1981 (as a successor to the old *Commoners' Newsletter*). This is edited, and often contributed to, by two Commoners, Charity Maudslay and Barbara Willard. Miss Willard is an elected Commoner and writer, whose knowledge of the Forest is profound and heartfelt.

Another source of current information, centred around Fairwarp and its church, is the monthly *Fairwarp Echo*. The editor of this enterprising little journal is Mrs Mary Threfeld of Duddleswell. Fairwarp was without a vicar the last time I was there, which posed problems for the parish during the inter-regnum.

During the period that this book was written there was at times an uneasy feeling of controversy within the Ashdown area, and at a Public Meeting held at the Roebuck, Wych Cross, in November 1981 some disapproval was expressed of the activities of the Board of Conservators. This got into the national Press who immediately, with some inaccuracy, tried to report it as a 'Them and Us' situation.

Another Public Meeting followed in February 1982, at Nutley, at which members of the Board, including elected Commoners and Appointed County and District Councillors, explained the workings and rather complex finance, and this was considered generally to be a successful meeting.

I attended one of the two-monthly meetings of the Board myself in March 1982, and from it learnt that it would seem that the worst problems facing the Forest then were illegal horse-riding, sheep worrying, and damage to vegetation by excessive public use; all I thought difficult to control.

A background problem of course is the decline in grazing. There is now only one large flock of sheep, owned by Mr Henry Osborne of Misbourne Farm, a Commoner, whose farm is in the south of the open Forest area; Mrs Sheldrick's Jacobs and some sheep grazed by Mrs Court; and I believe one solitary cow. It is then somewhat ironical to find that further north in Yorkshire the famous Ilkley Moor is suffering from overgrazing by sheep, where farmers graze nearly 2,500, and the Commons commis-sioners have decided that 1,300 are enough. But even that is too high for Bradford Council, which is going to appeal to the High Court. Grazing of sheep is a recent common right, and dates only from 1900 on Ashdown Forest, and I wonder what would have happened to the vegetation had there been really heavy grazing.

The future of the Forest must be seen against the background of the nation as a whole, and the immediate surroundings of rural Sussex and Kent. It is not often realized that the popu-lation of Sussex increased only fourfold in 1,200 years, from the seventh century to 1801, when it was 160,000; since then it has increased eight times to over 1¼ millions, so Ashdown Forest in fact is an island of relative sparse population amid an overcrowded, heavily urbanized county. Much of the surrounding Weald is now farmed by distant institutional methods; and the small family farmer and even the large estate are declining in numbers. The outward movement of people from derelict inner cities to the ever-growing clean, but monotonous, suburbs, and then finally to escape urban life altogether by moving into the countryside, has brought great pressures on the so-called isolated areas of hitherto unspoilt and unfrequented rural landscapes of which Ashdown Forest is almost the last one left in south-eastern England.

Those that have come to, or near, Ashdown to live, and sometimes acquired rights of common (which they do not always seem to understand) then find that their rural isolation is often invaded, or so it seems to them, and naturally they want it kept exclusive. But Ashdown Forest is not just a place to walk dogs and admire the views. It is the last relic of the old Wealden Forest we have left, and is therefore unique and ought, with its wildlife, grazing and controlled horseriding, to be kept as wild as possible, with urban influences to a minimum. It is a question of balance, control and discipline, but unfortunately the nation has become almost anarchic in its reluctance to accept any form of restraint. Nowhere is this more marked than with car ownership, whose convenience has become a god, transcending all other modern aids to domestic and urban comfort, so much so that without it people feel helpless, lost and deprived.

If Ashdown is to remain as it is at present, then I suggest that only three main roads across it are necessary, the A22, the A26 and the A275. All others should be sealed at their entrances and exits from the Forest and treated as private roads for the use of residents, Rangers, the Army, medical and fire services, and comparable with the forest roads in the Forestry Commission estates and plantations. Draconian? Yes, but eventually it will become impossible to contain the car-borne visitors, and the Forest will be spoilt for everybody, not least the residents.

The need for this measure is urgent, because the biggest threat to the Forest is just over the borders at Crowborough and Horsted Keynes where seismic soundings have produced 'interesting' results according to the Canadian company who are now applying for licences to exploit the possible oil and gas beneath the Crowborough Anticline, which is part of the Wealden Dome.

It is no use pretending that this is something that can be prevented by local planning and public enquiries; if the oil is there these will be overruled by the Department of the Environment on grounds of expediency, and the need to balance our payments of imported food by oil exports, as is being done with North Sea oil at present. No political party really believes in the environment, they pay only lip service to it; Britain's recent history shows that with the Vale of Belvoir mining proposals and Cow Green Reservoir in the Midlands and the North.

As a nation we are proud of our countryside, but we do little really to protect it. I remember about a decade ago whilst travelling in the Loire Valley I met an old viticulteur at Pouilly of white wine fame. He was sticking his own labels on some bottles, and happened to mention he knew Tonbridge and the Weald. 'Some of the best countryside I've ever seen,' he said, 'but the changes are too swift and sudden for me to live there.'

The Forest as we know it could disappear by the end of the century, unless . . . and that could be up to the readers perhaps of this book.

Appendix—O.S. References for Wealden Ironworking Sites

	Reference
Prehistoric (Iron Age)	
Sandyden Ghyll	586–309
Minepit Wood	523–338
Cinderhill	380–298
Garden Hill(Ashdown)	444–319
ROMAN BLOOMERIES	
Ashdown Forest(Private)	
Garden Hill	444–319
Pippingford	446–313
Stickedridge Gill	456–317
Stony Gill(Cow Park)	452–309
Crabtree Farm	485–298
Oldlands	476–269
Pippingford(East Wood)	442–301
Fringe Areas(N. Slopes)	
Ridge Hill	369–359
Walesbeech(W. Wood)	395–345
Great Cansiron	448–382
Eridge(Old Park)	578–345
Cinder Wood	435–397
Eastern Ridges	
Brook House	506–273
Newnham Park	495–284
Oaky Wood	507–272
Front Wood	490–246

Greystones Farm	495–271
Morphews	509–256
Stilehouse Wood	585–303
Castle Hill	559–280
Sandyden Ghyll	586–309
Hodges Wood	527–326
Scaland Wood	523–277
Renby Grange	532–332
Limney	540–271
Colegrove	590–330
Ringles Farm	507–340
Chant Farm	559–304
Earlye Farm	598–329
Little Trodgers	590–300

Southern Villages

Hempstead Wood	490–216
Flat Farm	552–220
Bosmere Farm	545–222
Scocus Farm	552–231
Pounsley	525–220
Little Inwoods	562–240

SAXON BLOOMERY

Millbrook(Ashdown F.)	441–296

MEDIEVAL BLOOMERIES

Crowborough Common	509–277
Boardshead(near)	526–324
Orznash(north of)	523–338
Buxted	498–225
High Hurstwood(near)	504–251

TUDOR & LATER IRONWORKS
Ashdown Forest

Newbridge	456–325
Steel Forge(Pippingford)	449–315
Crowborough Warren Furnace	496–322
Mardon Hill Forge	499–326
Pippingford (1717 furns.)	450–316
Boringwheel Farm & Mill	456–264
Old Forge (Furnace & Forge)	459–258

Fringes(Northern Slopes)

Gravetye	Manor House
Mill Place	Farmhouse
Stone, East Grinstead	Weir Wood
Parrock	458–357
Chartness(Hartfield)	457–363
Withyham(Stonelands)	Buckhurst Park
Eridge (Old Forge)	560–351
Eridge Park (Furnace)	564–351
Birchden Forge	Stream spillway
Hamsell Furnace	Lake
Ashhurst Furnace	508–391
Ashhurst Forge	7/8 m.N.Ch.
Bower	440–384
Cansiron	453–382

Western Slopes

Strudgate Furnace	Lake
Chittingly Manor	Pond
Ardingly College(Furnace)	337–287
Horsted Keynes Furnace	Large Lake
Freshfield Forge	Sloop Inn

Eastern Ridges

Maynards Gate	540–298
Cowford	560–319
Henly	601–337
Riverhall	605–333
Mayfield Furnace	590–283
Mayfield Forge	594–281
Oldlands Furnace	477–272
Hendall Furnace	470–250
Huggets Furnace	535–260
Howbourn Forge	516–250

Southern Villages

Sheffield Park Forge	Railway Stn
Fletching Forge	Mill Farm(Ouse)
Maresfield Park(Forge)	456–231
Maresfield Park(Furnace)	Large lake
Pounsley Furnace	529–219
Newplace Farm(Framfield)	Lake

Index

Railways, 22, 26, 30, 41, 45, 53, 61,
  66, 68, 69, 74–5, 80, 82, 83, 86–7, 90,
  133, 136, 141, 142, 147, 149, 160,
  171, 185; Bluebell, 74–5, 86, 90;
  Brighton Line, 78, 80, 91; British,
  74, 86; Cuckoo Line, 53, 61, 68;
  Estate, 147; LBSCR, 26, 30, 45, 75,
  82, 83, 136; SER (Hastings), 56;
  Southern, 149
Redgate Mill, 53, 133, 134
Repton, Humphrey, 19, 76, 148, 169
riots, 1830, 36, 61, 64, 66–7
Riverhall, 54, 173–4
Rocks: Bowles, 48, 98; Eridge, 39;
  High, 31–2, 41; Stone Farm, 25; The
  (Uckfield), 70; Tudor, 51
Romans, 14, 53, 79, 80, 82, 99, 109,
  110–12, 115, 152, 157–61, 162;
  Emperors, 158; iron industry, 14,
  53, 79, 110, 152, 157–61, 162; roads,
  14, 80, 82, 110–12, 156; tiles, 158,
  159–60, 162; villas, 110, 158–9, 160
Rother, River, 42, 53, 58, 59, 61, 97,
  153, 173
Rotherfield, 36, 39, 42, 44, 45, 52–3,
  54, 55, 61, 130, 133, 168; Church,
  52–3, 133
Royal Forest, 15
Rye (Sussex), 152, 167

Sackvilles, 36–7, 114, 123, 128, 134,
  149; Colleges, 26, 36; Dukes of
  Dorset, 36, 125, 128, 132, 134; Earls
  de la Warr, 36–7, 43, 75, 93, 134,
  137–8, 146, 177, 180; Earls of
  Dorset, 36, 123, 124
St Dunstan, 59, 173
Saint Hill Green, 25
St Leonard's Forest, 11, 17–18, 163
Saxonbury Hill, 24, 54, 157
Saxons and Saxony, 12, 14, 15, 27, 80,
  112, 161; South, 14, 15, 80, 81, 100
Scottish and Scotland, 13, 64, 82, 119,
  162, 181, 193
Scrag Oak, 57–8
Selsfield, 80, 139
Seymour, Admiral Lord, 33, 167, 172
Shaw, Norman, 27
shaws and hedgerows, 17, 19, 20, 23,
  100, 184
sheep and sheep farming, 33, 35, 72,
  101, 120, 127, 137, 144, 154, 181,
  184, 195

Sheffield, 75, 156; Arms, 91; Bridge,
  74, 78
  Earls: 1st, 74, 75, 76, 91, 132, 134;
  2nd, 75; 3rd, 75, 76, 137, 155–6
  Forest, 76, 92, 172; forges and
  furnaces, 167, 172; Green, 91; Mill,
  167, 172; Park, 16, 49, 75–6, 155–6,
  167; Shield (cricket), 75
Shelley: Arms Inn, 127; family, 63,
  134, 137
Shepherd's Hill, 67
Silva Anderida, 14, 22, 89, 151
Sitwell, Sir Osbert, 26
smuggling, 17, 19–20, 25, 31, 44, 67,
  128–31
snakes, 191–3; adders, 179, 191,
  192–3
Snape Wood, 57, 155
South Frithe Forest, 116
Spanish and Spain, 33, 58, 92, 135,
  158
squatters, 43, 64, 102, 127, 138–9, 163
Steel Forge, River, 104, 111, 112, 141,
  153–4, 159; bloomeries, 159;
  furnaces, 163, 165–6
Straker, Ernest, 77, 84, 104, 160, 161,
  174, 175
submarines, 61, 191
Suntings Farm, 100
Surrey, 24, 26, 53, 128, 136, 146, 157
Sussex: Archaeological Society, 102,
  158; Naturalist's Trust, 143, 191;
  Ornithological Society, 187
Sweet Minepits, 124, 127

Tanks (military), 111, 142, 175, 187
Tebbutt, Mr C. F., 66, 77, 99, 108, 109,
  119, 159, 165
Teise, River, 14, 42, 53, 173
Thames, River, 31, 32, 95, 103, 108,
  128
Thompsett's Bank, 127, 138
Ticehurst, 17
Tilgate Stone, 18, 74, 80
Tonbridge, 24, 157, 175, 197
Trees:
  hardwoods: alder, 13, 54, 64, 67, 77,
    89, 98, 99, 127, 178, 188; ash, 19,
    20, 89, 113; beech, 11, 13, 19, 25,
    36, 38, 40, 67, 100, 102–3, 115,
    118, 172, 187; birch, 11, 12, 13, 51,
    54, 64, 68, 99, 100, 103, 118, 127,
    178, 181, 187; chestnuts and